Vilém Flusser

Philosophy of Language

Translated by Rodrigo Maltez Novaes

Flusser Archive Collection

Foreword by Sean Cubitt

- *Filosofia da linguagem,* 1965 -
© Copyright Miguel Gustavo Flusser

Translated from Portuguese by Rodrigo Maltez Novaes
as *Philosophy of Language*

First Edition
Minneapolis © 2016, Univocal Publishing

Published by Univocal
411 N. Washington Ave., STE 10
Minneapolis, MN 55401
www.univocalpublishing.com

This book has been published with support from the
Brazilian Ministry of Culture / National Library Foundation.

Obra publicada com o apoio do
Ministério da Cultura do Brasil / Fundação Biblioteca Nacional.

 MINISTÉRIO DA CULTURA
Fundação BIBLIOTECA NACIONAL

Thanks to Edith Flusser, Dinah Flusser, Miguel Gustavo Flusser,
the Vilém Flusser Archive at the Universität der Künste Berlin,
Daniel Irrgang, and Sean Cubitt

Designed & Printed by Jason Wagner
Distributed by the University of Minnesota Press

ISBN 9781937561536
Library of Congress Control Number 2016937983

Table of Contents

FLUSSER ARCHIVE COLLECTION

Vilém Flusser is one of the most influential thinkers of media and cultural theory as well as the philosophy of communication in the second half of the 20th century. But unlike certain thinkers of media culture such as Marshall McLuhan or Jean Baudrillard, most of his work has yet to attain the proper attention of the reading public inside and outside the walls of the academy. One of the reasons for this is due to the singular process by which Flusser constructed his thinking and writing. He is a rare polyglot who would write his texts in various languages until he was satisfied with the outcome. Fluent in Czech, German, French, English, and Portuguese, he has left an archive full of thousands of manuscripts in various languages. The Flusser Archive Collection will be a monumental step forward in finally providing an Anglophone readership with a collection of some of Flusser's most important works.

Translator's note

This book is a series of lectures that Flusser delivered at the Brazilian Institute of Philosophy (IBF), São Paulo, in 1963, and at the Institute of Technology for Aeronautics (ITA), São José dos Campos, in 1965. It was subsequently published in the ITA journal in 1965.

Originally, the series of lectures had seventeen planned sessions, but was stopped, for unknown reasons, after the tenth session. However, Flusser picked up the theme in another two series of lectures, also at the Brazilian Institute of Philosophy, in 1964 and 1965 respectively, where he expanded the theme and which were titled *Fundamental Concepts of Western Thought* and *The Influence of Existentialist Thought Today*. Both are also part of this series by Univocal Publishing.

PHILOSOPHY OF LANGUAGE

Foreword

So lucid is the prose of Vilém Flusser (and his translator Rodrigo Maltez Novaes) that a forward seems almost an impertinence. Some small contextual notes might perhaps help position these lectures. In 1963, Brazil was moving from a policy of intense inward investment by foreign capital to a government characterised by its proximity to the working class and traditional working class parties, including the Communists. In 1964 however, there would be a military junta which would hold power for over twenty years. The country's intellectual and artistic ferment in the years immediately preceding the junta can be evoked with a handful of names: Paulo Freire, Hélio Oiticica, Lygia Clark, Augusto Boal, Nelson Pereira dos Santos, Ruy Guerra, Glauber Rocha…. As a member of the organizational committee of the São Paulo Biennial, Flusser was in contact with the vivid art scene as well as the major intellectual currents of his adopted home.

He was also blessed and cursed with what he described in an essay as "the freedom of the migrant": a freedom that allows the incomer a cold analysis of their adopted home while keeping them at arm's length from it. Though constantly offering dialogue with colleagues in São Paulo, Flusser's major references are to Europe, and to a Europe already, by 1963, just a little passé in European eyes (as when he mentions only just having come across Claude Lévi-Strauss, ten years after the popular success in France of *Tristes Tropiques*, largely about indigenous Brazilian tribes). Instead these lectures dive backwards from the existentialism of Camus and Sartre towards the phenomenological studies of Heidegger and Husserl, a trajectory he suggests was to lead deeper into the history of philosophy in the next year's lecture series. There is here evidence of a mixed condition: on the one hand, of isolation from the structuralist currents sweeping Europe at the time, and on the other a freedom from their more doctrinaire or merely fashionable domination. He was able therefore to develop a startlingly independent investigation into the linguistic turn of both continental and Anglo-Saxon traditions in the early and mid 20th century.

As with so many of the great thinkers, it is not only what Flusser thinks but how he thinks that is of value. In elegant, almost languid reflections, he undertakes reflection on key terms like "proper name" and "self" to bring his readers to reorient themselves to over-familiar positions concerning his central topics, meaning and truth. In the wake of Wittgenstein, Saussure and post-structuralism, the claim that language constructs reality is no longer as shocking as it was; but to have developed this thesis independently of European structuralism, and by such an original route, is one of Flusser's achievements. That would however only be of interest to historians if the originality of his argument did not bring us first to quizzing the mythic basis of the proper name, in which language expresses the unique event of its encounter with the world, his prescription of poetry as the proper elaboration of such encounters, and science as the process of converting that poetry into prose, a process in which the richness of meaning is gradually scrubbed away until nothing is left: a nothing which, however, it is our unique historical task, as moderns, to confront.

This utterly inadequate (and slightly incorrect) account of Flusser's argument is intended not to pre-empt reading this extraordinary little book, but on the contrary, to encourage a reading of it in tune with Flusser's pedagogic circumstance. These are lectures, for students, which connect outwards to other lectures by other professors. They are in that sense centrifugal. While they articulate a very clear argument, they also operate as stimulants for other enquiries, in their provocations (starting with the description of philosophy as "small talk" on page 2) and in the manner of their logic. Given the premise that "everything that is not linguistic is absurd" (p.10), and given the caveat that not everything linguistic is meaningful, both the creativity and the responsibilities of speaking and writing become central, not only to his own thought but to the stimulation of thinking in his students. Like Adorno's "The Essay as Form", originally written in the late 1950s, Flusser's lectures give pride of place to the unique moment in which world and self mutually form one another in the proper name; and see only decline in the movement from the unique to the general and universal for which he reserves the term "common name." Knowledge, Flusser argues, "is ontologically anterior to knower and known. Knower and known are the two aspects and the two horizons of knowledge … intellect and external world are the two aspects and the two horizons of language." Self, reality, and their relation as meaning exist in and because of their co-constitution in the unique, unrepeatable event of their encounter in the plane of language, which is not the sole property of either (and is therefore no more the mathematics of nature than it is the syntax of reason).

If in this momentous collision of modes of being we can catch a hint of Badiou's philosophy of the Event, it may suggest not only that there is a dynamic running through the Brazilian exile and the Parisian post-Maoist; but that there is also a political dynamic which remains to be released from Flusser's thinking, which has occasionally been seen as apolitical or even conservative. On the one hand, it might suggest, as critics of Badiou have done (Papadopoulos et al 2008), that new generations should be impatient of their elders who assert that the event, on which whatever truth we have is founded, is always in the past. At the same time, Flusser points beyond Badiou's ethics of fidelity to a past event, and towards a more 21st century conception of mediation as the central fact of human being, mediations that in fact explode the concept of self and world by envisaging both as horizons not only of language and meaning but of the asignifying flux of ecological entanglement.

In this sense, although Flusser begins from phenomenology, he leads towards aesthetics. The step is a small one: phenomenology is the philosophy of experience; aesthetics that of the senses, though it became in modern times the philosophy of beauty in particular and thence of art. The ancient Greeks had no word for communication. Instead poetics, rhetoric and aesthetic philosophy

XII

in their time – and into Roman classicism and mediaeval theology – engaged with the issues we today address as communication (Peters 1999). Even though his subject is language, Flusser's approach is phenomenological at root, dealing with the sensory immersion in the world that constitutes the poetic moment that requires, as the only adequate response, a proper name: the name, we might say, of a god whose invocation is enough to call to mind the sheer otherness of a storm, a river or a mountain. Yet while he suggests such moments are foundational, he also asserts that they are continuous. In this way he reflects a major preoccupation of his contemporaries like Ricœur and Merleau-Ponty with the non-verbal aspects of human experience. Since Flusser is in many circles best known for his work on photography, it is worth suggesting here that these lectures already suggest that language may not be restricted to the verbal, but might also include the figurative arts.

Contemporary phenomenologists of media like Vivian Sobchack (2004) point towards the expansion of definitions of self required once we broach the borders of the linguistic. Perhaps because he was outside the sphere of structuralist influence, Flusser never subordinates the other media to language, and so allows the bodily movement of images, sounds, shapes and textures to approach the world in parallel with language, without language's tendency to reduce the particular to the universal, the unique to the general. The potential for wonder is constant. And yet we are constantly vulnerable, as Ricœur (1977: 365) would argue a decade after Flusser, to the mismatch between lived experience and linguistic expression, in the kind of lazy metaphor that forces words to extend beyond their referent and so lose touch with that of which they were to have been the expression. Science and reason triumph over poetry to the degree that they remain more true to that initial expression, since Pythagoras first established the mathematical forms of music, because in avoiding the temptation of metaphor they retain the truth that "It is Pan's flute that establishes, with its mathematical harmony, what we call 'reality.'" (109). As mathematics, music retains its proximity to that more embodied experience of the event in which world and self are generated, the event whose name is, if not that of a god like Pan, at least that of a specific moment rather than a generic one. It is only in logic and in discourse that we lose this specificity. To the extent that it retains its music, poetry is a saving grace, since "What is not ours within the verse is its vibration with nothingness. This enigmatic quality of the verse is its meaning" (136). Vibration, the harmony of poetry and whatever is beyond the human, preserves within its otherwise linguistic form its capacity to convey the enigma of the void. And ironically, it is the loss of this enigma that creates absurdity, since the meaning of poetry is precisely what exceeds and escapes language, since everything that is wholly encompassed within language can no longer be meaningful. We can only conclude that the phenomenological body itself is external to language and therefore also within the enigma, and that the senses and the media that speak to them for that reason are not caught in the entropic decline towards absurdity.

In this way Flusser helps to indicate a vital feature of the human experience: that it is indeed linguistic, and bonded through language to logic and reason, but that it is simultaneously married to the enigma of non-existence through the communicative capability of the body. On the one hand human experience is exclusively human to the extent that it is in a continuum with language; while on the other its communicative capability lies in its embodiment, which it shares with the rest of the world, and which thereby becomes the channel of the enigmatic co-existence of being and non-being, unity and multiplicity. The essential connection Flusser establishes between the phenomenal – human experience – and the communicative – which is also common to animals and environments – is already ecological. This is of a part with his post-Freudian understanding of the self as a fluid construct dependent on language and therefore not self-founding or isolated, but already constructed by the language which connects it to other living creatures. If however communication exceeds language to include all the senses, then those connections do not stop with human beings but extend outward to the flora and fauna, the biosphere and geology of the planet, and beyond it to the moon and sun and the longer, slower, vaster interactions of all of these with the cosmos beyond.

If this seems too fantastical, consider the pages Flusser devotes here to the study of myth. Here the ground of being is non-existence. There is a huge difficulty here, because as Flusser observes, the Western tradition is entirely devoted to the pursuit of being and beings, to Leibniz' question "why is there something rather than nothing." Flusser's reply, echoing the Eastern tradition, is that there is nothing. But what is this nothing? It is what precedes language, meaning, and the objectification of objects they bring. Myth is how poetry extracts something from nothingness, "somethings" whose being is intrinsically mythical since they have no prior existence, yet which bear precious and unrepeatable truths of the encounter with that nothingness that precedes and encircles human being. "Today," he tells us, "ontology is, in the end, mythology." It is the confrontation not with being but with nothing. The mathematical philosophers since Frege and Cantor have also explored this mythic boundary of thought. Observing that, in the founding axioms of logic and ontology, everything that exists is identical to itself $(A = A)$, Frege defined zero as that which is not identical to itself and therefore does not exist. As the non-identical, zero configures that universal multiplicity and instability that persists through its sheer incapacity to exist, its lack of being. Establishing a logical proof that all numbers derive from zero, logic demands recognition that non-identity lurks in every constructed identity: every unity is haunted by multiplicity and flux. Such, it may be, is the substantive nothing that Flusser engages. What persists without existing and lies beyond and within language and reason? What grounds and escapes human existence? In Flusser's exploration of language I believe we hear the beginnings of a 21st century analysis which holds that what escapes and grounds us simultaneously is the mediation which under other discourses we know as ecology. This is the implication of his philosophy of conversation, evolved and developed in Chapters VII and VIII here.

It is odd, on the face of it, that at the very moment he asserts that Western scientific rationality has exhausted

XVI

its role of doubting the truths of poetry and must pass on to the next generation, Flusser moves towards history. We might, in retrospect look back to the 1960s, to the failure in Brazil of the model of development through mechanisation and industrialisation, to the waning of the language of mechanical engineering as the discourse not only of policy but of architects and cultural visionaries, and its replacement by variants of network emergence as core trope, from ecological science to neo-liberalism, and from Ted Nelson to Gilles Deleuze. But that seems to give Flusser less than his due, and to leave opaque his historiographic tactic. To get some inkling of what he might have intended, and to see what legacy he has left for us, we need to take another look at the dialectical turns in his argument. Thought, he argues, "is a negating and negative process. What thought negates is the nothingness that proper names signify. Thought is a process that negates nothingness." As progressive doubt applied to the initial mythic confrontation with nothingness as non-identity, thought neutralises the *horror vacui* but at the same time denudes the god named by that event by normalising it as common, general, universal and therefore whole. The crisis of metaphor is its decline into the common name.

Flusser tactically moves into the past as a way of working his way back up the entropic slope of language towards its beginning in poetry. We should consider this in terms of the crisis which was already beginning to engulf Brazil in 1963, a political crisis of course, but one propelled by the upshot of inward investment: debt. Debt, which has become the name of the central crisis of the early 21st century, is just such a failed metaphor. In its roots it denotes an obligation to the past: a debt owed to ancestors, to the generosity of the sun and earth and stars. In its new conformation, it denotes a payment due to an indefinitely postponed future. This reversal of polarity has in many respects poisoned the orientation of hope for a future radically different to the past by condemning the indebted, which included Brazil and now includes every nation and most individuals, to reproducing their labour and the social organisation that goes with it until that impossible moment in which all debts are reconciled. To return to the past is not a mark of defeat but a tactical withdrawal designed to draw strength from that suppressed but vitally contemporary time he calls "illo tempore", the moment of confrontation in which world and self are made new. These lectures illuminate the idea of truth in language by pointing towards its profoundly temporal structure, and in turning to the past, make the future, as the domain of hope, possible again.

Sean Cubitt

References

Adorno, Theodor W. (1984). "The Essay as Form". Trans Bob Hullot-Kentor and Frederic Will. New German Critique, 32, Spring - Summer. 151-171; reprinted in Adorno, Theodor W. (1991). Notes to Literature, volume 1. Trans Shierry Weber Nicholsen. New York: Columbia University Press. 3-23.

Papadopolos, Dimitiris, Niamh Stephenson and Vasilis Tsianos (2008). *Escape Routes: Control and Subversion in the Twenty-first Century.* London: Pluto.

Peters, John Durham (1999). *Speaking into the Air: A History of the Idea of Communication.* Chicago: University of Chicago Press.

Ricœur, Paul (1977). *The Rule of Metaphor: The creation of meaning in language.* Trans Robert Czerny with Kathleen McLaughlin and John Costello, SJ. London: Routledge.

Sobchack, Vivian, (2004). "What My Fingers Knew: The Cinesthetic Subject, or Vision in the Flesh". *Carnal Thoughts: Embodiment and Moving Image Culture.* Berkeley: University of California Press. 53-84.

I. Philosophy as the Critique of Language

We have gathered for a series of lectures that are, for me, a promise of adventure. I would propose to lay bare the basic lines of what I could call "how I conceive the world," if that were not so intolerably pretentious, not only in relation to myself, but also in relation to the world. Effectively, I propose to elucidate, in this course of lectures, not only to you but also to myself, some points that seem to me both basic and obscure. I have, obviously, an approximate program of what I shall submit to your critique, but this program is only rough. It is, as they say in Existential philosophy, a "project"; a project I sought to realize several times, with varying results. Results depend on the forces that converge upon them, and in this case, they depend upon you and me. That is why I have said that this series contains, for me, a promise of adventure. I cannot know in which direction your critiques will canalize the course of my argument. I shall prepare every individual lecture in response to the preceding discussion. I am therefore grateful to you for this opportunity, since I have never been able to discuss my thoughts with a group like the one present here.

What we are getting ready to do is called "philosophy" (maybe with excessive elegance). I propose, as an "*hors d'oeuvre*" of this course, the discussion of this activity sometimes called "philosophy." If we seek a distanced point of view, in order to observe this activity, if philosophy is an external object, of which we are subjects, it will present itself as a member of that class of activities called "small talk." From this phenomenological distance, where we suspend all previous knowledge that we may possibly have in relation to philosophy, it presents itself as an activity that consists of the reading of books, the discussion of such readings in groups of people generally gathered together in classrooms, and, sometimes, the elaboration of works written about such readings; works to be published in order to be read and discussed, and so on and so forth "*ad nauseam*" and "*ad infinitum*." One cannot observe, in this phenomenological "*époche*" which we assume at this moment any, let us say, graspable effect of this activity. Philosophy is a purely linguistic activity: a chitchat that has words as an instrument, words as a subject, and words as an aim. Husserl believes that this distance, which we assume, is a symptom of our humility, and that philosophy, that is, the phenomenon before which we are humbling ourselves, thus reveals its essence, its "*eidos*." Philosophy's "*eidos*" is small talk. However, phenomenology's humility is the highest form of pride. If we observe philosophy from this angle of pretend innocence and ignorance, we shall be underrating the phenomenon before which we pretend to humble ourselves. In order to be itself, philosophy does not admit distance, but demands engagement. It is only through dedicated and integral engagement that philosophy will slowly reveal its essence, an essence that I do not hesitate to call "beauty." We must therefore say

2

that philosophy does not reveal itself to the distant and patient observer, but to the interested and impassioned participant.

However, it is obvious that the distance, which revealed to us that philosophy is a type of small talk, is a perfectly legitimate and epistemologically pertinent point of view (although perhaps existentially impertinent). Somehow, this point of view relates to philosophy. To really philosophize is to read, to write, to talk to others, and to talk to oneself through that internal dialogue that Plato called thinking. Philosophy is a linguistic activity, which takes place entirely on the terrain of written, spoken, or internally whispered language. Philosophy is a conversation. And it is a curious type of conversation, since its discourse flows, but does not progress (as for example, the scientific discourse progresses), nor does it manipulate objects (as for example, that discourse called art, manipulates). In my view, Dilthey is profoundly wrong in wanting to transform philosophy into a science of the spirit, because philosophy is structurally an unprogressive discourse.

Marx is equally wrong, in my view, in proclaiming that philosophy only explains the world, when what really matters is to modify the world. Philosophy is structurally non-manipulative. A scientific philosophy, and a philosophy engaged in the Marxist sense, has already stopped being philosophy "*eo ipso.*" Given philosophy's unprogressive and non-manipulative character, it is therefore perfectly legitimate to call it small talk.

Let us consider, for one instant, the concept of "small talk" that I am employing here. Small talk is a type of conversation in which phrases flow just for the sake of flowing, without aiming at something external to the conversation. In small talk one speaks for the sake of speaking, without an external aim to the conversation. Small talk has no external subject; small talk is its own subject. A conversation that aims at an external aim, signifies such aim, and that aim is its meaning. Small talk has no meaning. But small talk is composed – like every conversation – of phrases, which are, respectively, composed of words. Words are signs of something; they mean something. Within small talk, their meanings are as if forgotten, swallowed up by the small talk itself. What matters in small talk is not the words' meaning, but the words themselves. To say that philosophy is small talk is to say that it lacks meaning.

Let us take, as an example of small talk, exchanges at the food market, and demagogy. The orange seller who articulates phrases whose words signify the buyer's health, and the speaker at the political rally who articulates phrases whose words signify the country's debt, are not interested in the meaning of their words. Nonetheless, they still seek an external aim to small talk, that is, to sell oranges or canvass votes. These unconfessed and disguised aims become the meaning of small talk. Small talk lacks meaning if taken literally, but is full of meaning within a wider existential context. Small talk distinguishes itself from its opposite by its insincerity. Small talk is inauthentic conversation, because it has a meaning that is not the meaning of the words it employs. To say that philosophy is small talk is to say that it is formally meaningless, but that it has an unconfessed meaning. Can we pass such a merciless sentence upon philosophy?

Yes we can, since the two most characteristic currents of contemporary philosophy mutually judge each other thus. I am referring to that tendency vaguely called "Neopositivism" and to that other known by the dubious term "Existentialism." Under a logical analysis (Neopositivism's main weapon), practically every phrase articulated by the existentialists is revealed as pure meaningless noise. The aim of Existentialism cannot, therefore, be the meaning of its phrases, but another, unconfessed aim. Existentialism is small talk. Under an existentialist analysis, practically every phrase articulated by the neopositivists obviously has a meaning that is not the meaning of the words employed. Effectively, neopositivist texts are nothing but precious and presumptuous pretexts meant to avoid the direct confrontation of the mind with the existential situation in which it finds itself. Neopositivism is small talk. And if we were to reduce the phrases that make up the discourse of the philosophy of the past to their logico-symbolic or their existential climate, we would verify that they are, almost all of them, small talk. And the few phrases that could be saved from a logico-symbolic point of view, will be unmasked as existentially false, and the remaining few that are existentially sincere, will not resist a neopositivist formal analysis. In other words: the phrases that compose philosophy's discourse are either mere sentimental exclamations without formal meaning, or pretentious formalism meant to hide existential angst, or both. Philosophy is, therefore, small talk.

Having passed such a condemning sentence, I ask myself, deeply shocked: what would be an example of non-small talk? Obviously a conversation whose meaning is the meaning of the words that it employs. So let us search for this type of antithetical conversation so that we may engage with it, and let us abandon *incontinenti* the insincerities and noises of philosophy. Let us take the two examples opposite to philosophy already mentioned, that is, science and art. Obviously, science is a conversation that is accepted as meaningful by the neopositivists, at least in theory. Its phrases resist logical analysis, and when they do not, they are happily abandoned by science in its progress. And it is equally obvious that the meaning of science is that external situation that the scientific words signify, in other words, "the world." Both of these points are obvious, but both contain, if patiently analyzed, grave problems. Let us ignore this. However, if seen from an existential angle, how does science present itself? It presents itself as uniquely, gigantically, and monumentally insincere. It pretends that the logical intellect is able to grasp the totality, or parcels, of what we call "reality," even when authentic immediate experience contradicts this pose at every step. And science pretends that man has the power to overcome the situation in which he was thrown, even when death contradicts this pose at every instant.

Effectively, science is nothing but small talk, whose unconfessed meaning is the attempt to forget the absurdity of the human condition.

Let us consider art. Obviously, for Existentialism, artistic activity is a manifestation of Man's own authenticity. Man realizes himself, as existence, through art, and imposes his way of being upon the circumstance in which he was thrown. Therefore, artistic existence is perfectly meaningful, although a more careful consideration may reveal grave problems. Let us ignore this. However, from a formal point of view, how does art present itself? What is the meaning of a poem, of a symphony, or of a painting? It certainly is not the meaning of the words, of the sounds, or of the paints that compose the work. They have another, unconfessed meaning. A formal analysis will reveal that art is nothing but a unique, gigantic, and monumental kind of small talk, formally equivalent in every way to the bray of an ass.

The two examples cited are enough to curtail our enthusiasm, and to encourage us to abandon philosophy and dive into some other type of conversation. What do these two examples suggest? That every conversation is small talk, if observed from an ironic point of view, that is, a distanced and unengaged point of view. And, "*mutatis mutandis,*" that every conversation, in which we engage existentially, with body and soul, is fully meaningful. However, philosophy differs from other types of conversation, because it is aware of this fact.

Effectively: philosophy is a linguistic activity that distinguishes itself from every other linguistic activity (such as science and art, for example) by its lack of naivety in relation to the meaning of human activity. That, which we call the philosophical spirit is, essentially, the loss of our naive faith in the meaning of human activity. Or, to reformulate, we may say that philosophy is an activity that seeks this lost meaning. The term "meaning" is, therefore, in my view, philosophy's key term, and therefore, also that of this series of lectures. The meaning of the term "meaning" varies according to the context in which the term is applied. To attempt to give a definition of this term would be, therefore, to define this course. Given the fluidity of my program, I am incapable, at this point, to give a definition of its key term. But as every conversation must use at least approximately defined terms in order to be understood, I propose the following operative definition, until otherwise defined: Meaning is that something, which signs aim at. If you accept this definition "for the duration," we shall have established the fundament from which our arguments will develop into unknown territory.

Only signs are meaningful. A situation that does not contain signs is meaningless. A situation that does not contain signs is absurd because it is meaningless. What we call "world," that is, the situation into which we have been thrown, will have meaning if it has signs, and if it does not, it will be absurd. Everything we do and suffer in this world, in synthesis, our life, will be meaningful as long as it relates to signs, and it will be absurd if it does not relate to signs. Signs are what introduce us to meaning; however, they conceal that meaning for the same reason. In this sense, signs are enigmatic. The world, and our existence within it, will be meaningful if they contain enigmatic elements, and if not, they will also be absurd. Signs can be grouped into systems that will be called "languages," during this course. Languages are systems of signs, and from now on signs within languages shall be called "symbols." A situation is meaningful when it contains signs, and it is an ordered situation when it has symbols contained in languages.

Given these definitions, which are amplifications of the operative definition of the term "meaning," I return to the theme of the consideration of philosophy. I have said that every linguistic activity presents itself as small talk, if observed from without, and as authentic conversation, if seen from the participant's perspective. Now I reformulate: Linguistic activity, if observed from without, presents itself as a collection of false symbols, that is, of meaningless symbols, because these symbols are not enigmatic to those who are not engaged in such activity. The same activity, if observed from within, presents itself as authentic conversation, because it consists of genuine symbols. I shall have the opportunity, in the course of these lectures, to elaborate upon these points. Philosophy differs from other activities because it is the only one that observes itself from within. Science and art, to persist with these two examples, are linguistic activities that start from symbols in order to develop them according to the rules of their respective languages. Philosophy is a linguistic activity that turns toward the symbol to discover the symbol's meaning. This is what we mean when we say that philosophy is reflexive. The movement of every linguistic activity's discourse is progressive; philosophy's movement is regressive. Because of its structure, philosophy is a linguistic movement that is opposed to the rest, and effectively, it drives against the others in order to reveal their meaning. Because of its structure, philosophy is a critique of linguistic activities, and the term "philosophy of language" is, in my opinion, a pleonasm. It is not experienced as a pleonasm because, given our naivety in relation to meaning, we are not always aware that everything that is not linguistic, is absurd. Philosophy as the critique of language, therefore, philosophy "*tout court*," will be the theme of this course of lectures.

Philosophy turns toward the symbol to discover the symbol's meaning. Within this turn resides philosophy's loss of naivety. The other linguistic activities (which I shall call from now on "progressive thought"), naively and uncritically accept the meaning of the symbols with which they operate. Progressive thought naively and indubitably accepts that symbols (which I shall "generally" call "concepts") seek something external to themselves, that is, "reality," and they progress from such premise. Only philosophy doubts this premise. Progressive thought accepts the enigmatic character of its own elements without critique; they do not frighten it. Philosophy faces this enigmatic character of symbols, and this is what the ancients meant when they said that fright is the beginning of philosophy. Aristotle said: "*propter admirationem enim et nunc et primo homines principiabant philosophari*" (it is through fright[1] that men started to philosophize, now and in the past). Because it is reflexive and regressive, philosophy is an activity that confronts what is frightening. And this fright, which philosophy is, only extinguishes itself when the philosopher believes to have discovered that symbols do not conceal anything. In this discovery of nothingness, fright transforms itself into a sensation of absurdity and

---

1. In Portuguese Flusser specifically uses the term *espanto*, which translates to English as "fright" instead of *admiração*, which would translate as the common rendering of *admirationem*, "wonder." [TN]

futility. This is the case of both Camus and Kafka. And Wittgenstein formulates it in a definitive manner: "there is no enigma." The discovery of nothingness behind the symbol is the discovery of the tautology of language. Language as a tautological system would be language as a system of empty symbols, and therefore false. Given our definition of meaning, this would imply an absurd world and the absurdity of the human situation. As paradoxical as it may seem, both Existentialism and Neopositivism seem to point toward this terribly unbearable result. The loss of naive faith in the meaning of symbols, which is the starting point of philosophy, seems to want to result in the discovery of total absurdity. This would not only be the end of philosophy, but also of every activity of thought. It would be the end of that conversation called "Western civilization," since, through philosophy, this conversation would recognize itself as small talk. The conclusion would be the Wittgensteinian one: "Whereof one cannot speak, thereof one must be silent."

The aim of this course of lectures will be to combat this result. I shall seek to demonstrate, both from a formal and an existential point of view, that the enigma of symbols, which are the elements of our thought, is inexhaustible. I shall seek to demonstrate that the conversation called "Western civilization" is not fated to fall into mutism, from either a formal or existential perspective, even though this fall is perfectly possible. I shall seek this aim via three distinct paths. I shall first seek to formally analyze our thought as a linguistic activity that develops within the field of particular languages. Following that, I shall seek to analyze this activity from an existential perspective, that is, as the progressive realization of a project contained within our languages. And lastly, I shall seek to illustrate this progressive realization within the course of Western history. Therefore, appealing to the terminology of classical philosophy, I shall first apply pure reason followed by practical reason, and lastly, historical reason, to the analysis of the situation in which we find ourselves. Therefore, I ask for your collaboration in this program.

My conviction, which I shall seek to defend, and to which I shall seek to convert you through an effort of proselytism, is the following: the sciences, the arts, and the religions, in sum, all forms of mental activity, are the progressive elaboration of symbols, which serve as elements of this activity. Symbols may, therefore, become extinguished. In being elaborated, these symbols transform the dormant potentialities within them into realities. Today, the physical sciences verge on this ultimate elaboration. They have transformed their symbols into instruments. These symbols are, therefore, no longer enigmatic, and the world of physics has been transformed into an absurd set of theories. Parallel to this, and by anticipating the results, other conversations are also threatened to fall into the absurdity of small talk. However, philosophy's role is precisely to counteract this advance. Its duty is to discover the inextinguishable enigma that are the primordial symbols, and to demonstrate that the realization reached, is only partial and imperfect. In other words, philosophy's role is to renew the sensation of fright before the enigmatic world that surrounds us. Thus renewed, philosophy will give a "new" meaning to human life. For whoever engages in thought through body and soul, to think, is not necessarily small talk. On the contrary, it is the constant discovery of enigma as the fundament of thought. This discovery is what I called "beauty," and it is to such frightening beauty, which philosophy discovers, if it is honest, that I invite you.

II. Pure Reason as the Structure of Language

During my introductory lecture, I said that the fright before the situation in which man finds himself, is the reason for philosophy. And this is true both from a historical and biographical perspective. However, from a methodological perspective, the moment of fright is not a good entry point for philosophy. As you know, the philosophical discipline is classified according to the themes from which it discourses. These classifications have a didactic aim and serve to teach philosophy, although they are not good for teaching how to philosophize. Therefore, these classifications vary according to the pedagogical prejudices of the classifiers. My own prejudices suggest the following classification:

1) Theory of knowledge
2) Theory of Being
   (a) Ontology
   (b) Cosmology
   (c) The analysis of existence
   (d) Theology

3) Theory of how things should be
      (a) Ethics
      (b) Legal philosophy
      (c) Aesthetics
      (d) Art philosophy
4) Theory of becoming
      (a) The philosophy of nature
      (b) The philosophy of science
      (c) The philosophy of history and culture
      (d) Philosophical anthropology
      (e) The philosophy of society, economy, religion etc.
5) Theory of thought
      (a) Logic
      (b) Mathematics
      (c) Philosophical psychology

I confess that this classification is artificial and that it imposes itself upon philosophy like a straitjacket. We shall not submit to it during this course of lectures. It will serve merely as a starting point. I shall begin my considerations within the field of what I have defined as "theory of knowledge." Modern philosophy, since the Renaissance, oscillates between two extremes within this field, called "Rationalism" and "Empiricism." "*Paucis verbis,*" both positions affirm the following:

Rationalism: Knowledge is a function of reason and consists of judgments. These judgments transform the confused raw material, which is indistinct from that dubious environment called "external world," into clear and distinct realities. Within knowledge, the external world becomes realized. Knowledge is the rationalization, that is, the humanization, of the external world. We may distinguish three historical phases within this position. First phase: There is an abyss between reason and the external world, which God helps to overcome. With God's help the external world may become completely known, that is, transformed into clear and distinct judgments. The representatives of this phase are Descartes, Spinoza, Leibniz, and Wolff. Second phase: Because it is in opposition to reason, the external world is nothing but a shadow of the reason that reason itself projects. Knowledge progressively enlightens this shadow and will end up recognizing itself in the shadow. In the last stage, the external world will have been overcome by reason, that is, everything will be reason, and nothing will be the external world. The representatives of this phase are Hegel, Marx (by inversion), and Positivism. Third phase: Because the external world is in opposition to reason, it cannot be touched by reason. The judgments formulated by reason cannot carry knowledge of the external world. They are intellectual phenomena and cannot overcome the intellect. Knowledge, if there is any, is not articulable. The intellect seeks in vain to break its shackles. The intellect is not an adequate instrument for the external world. The representatives of this phase are the neopositivists. From initial optimism through to final pessimism, there is one element that binds all rationalists: the aim toward clarity and distinction, the standard of which is mathematics or logic.

Empiricism: Knowledge is a function of experience and consists in the intellectual organization of impressions received by the intellect. Historically, Empiricism is a reaction to Rationalism, and always conserves this polemic and negative character. The intellect is a *tabula rasa*. It is an empty place upon which the external world impresses itself. It has no autonomy. Knowledge is an organized impression that the intellect has. The organization of this impression is due to the repetitive character of the external world. Experiences repeat and cause the impression of knowledge. The value of knowledge is only practical, since it provokes an adequate behavior in beings that possess intellect. The intellect is an instrument of these beings, just as gills and trunks are instruments of other beings. Knowledge is not an end-in-itself, but only the means. There is no such thing as knowledge itself; knowledge is only an impression. The representatives of this position are Locke, Hume, Schopenhauer, Nietzsche, Bergson, Kierkegaard, the Existentialists, and Pragmatism. Empiricism always tends toward skepticism and anti-intellectualism. It always appeals to raw and concrete experience, be it sensible, vital, or manipulable. Both positions, although opposites, lead to an either confessed or unconfessed despair in relation to the possibility of knowledge. However, it is obvious that something is wrong in the dichotomy that they establish. Science, which discourses within the terrain put in parentheses by the two extreme positions, ignores the fundamental objections hurled at it by them. It synthesizes rational and empirical elements and produces a growing body of knowledge, both theoretical and practical, to challenge philosophy. Therefore, attempts to synthesize these extreme positions have also been philosophically undertaken. The most important one was the Kantian. The Kantian position is this: The external world impresses itself upon reason, and in this sense the empiricists are correct. But reason is not empty, and in this sense they are wrong. It has, on the contrary, a structure called categories. At first, due to its structure, reason receives the impressions in two ways: time and space. And then, reason organizes these impressions, called "phenomena," into several compartments of its structure, which are: 1) unity, plurality, and totality 2) reality, negation, and limitation 3) substance and accident, cause and effect, and reciprocity 4) possibility, existence, and necessity. Due to these compartments called categories, reason organizes phenomena into judgments as knowledge. These judgments may be classified from two points of view. The first distinguishes between analytic and synthetic judgments; the second between *a priori* and *a posteriori* judgments. Analytic judgments predicate something contained in the subject, for example: "green grass, is green." Synthetic judgments predicate something not contained in the subject, for example: "the green grass is in the garden." *A priori* judgments result from the simple application of categorical rules, for example: "one is not two." *A posteriori* judgments do not apply these rules, for example: "yesterday it rained." It is obvious, given the Kantian definition of reason, that only *a priori* judgments produce knowledge, and that only synthetic judgments help knowledge to progress. In order to have knowledge, we need to have synthetic judgments *a priori*. Both Rationalism and Empiricism deny this possibility. Rationalism says that all of our judgments are either analytic *a priori*, therefore tautological, or synthetic *a posteriori*, therefore noise. Empiricism says that all of our judgments are either synthetic *a posteriori*, therefore instruments of behavior, or analytic *a priori*, therefore mere diversion. In the end, Rationalism and Empiricism agree. Kant affirms that synthetic *a priori* judgments do exist, and that they are the judgments of mathematics. "Two plus two equals four" is a synthetic judgment because the predicate "four" is not contained in the subject "two plus two," and it is *a priori* because it obeys the categorical rules. Science produces knowledge because it turns phenomena into mathematical judgments. *Quod erat demonstrandum.*

The Kantian argument, as genius as it is in its multiple aspects, seems particularly weak in its premises. What happens if we invert the *a priori* synthetic judgment and say, "four is two plus two"? Does it not become analytic, since "two plus two" is contained in "four"? But let us ignore that. What is shocking in Kant is the aleatory character of the categories that supposedly form the structure of pure reason. How did Kant arrive at the discovery of precisely these categories, and not others? Kant confesses. His categories emerged from a table of judgments that he elaborated and which consist of four groups of three types of judgments. The first relates to quantity, the second to quality, the third to relation, and the fourth to modality. But how did this table of judgments emerge? Kant falls silent. However, it is obvious how it emerged. The Kantian types of judgments are the result of the syntax of phrases. Effectively: from a syntactical analysis of phrases of the German language and similar languages. To begin with, the first two forms of receiving impressions ("*Anschauungsformen*"), which refer to space and time, correspond to substantives and verbs. And the categories are nothing but grammatical forms of languages of a certain type. Far from becoming the structure of pure reason "*tout court*," the forms, and the Kantian categories are, if Kant is right, only the categories of a particular type of languages.

I took Kant as the starting point for my considerations because Kant seems to be the only possibility to avoid the madness of skepticism. Let us see therefore, what may be salvaged from the Kantian system. Kant agrees with the radical rationalists that the external world cannot be intellectually reached. The thing-in-itself is unreachable by pure reason. It definitively proves, to me, that any metaphysical attempt is condemned to failure, at least intellectually. Hegelianism, Marxism, and Positivism seem to be a relapse into a pre-Kantian stage of philosophy. Neopositivism is, in this sense, a recovery. And Kant also proved definitively, to me, that this limitation of the intellect has skepticism as a necessary consequence. Knowledge is possible within a restricted field that is hermetically sealed. But not in the way that Kant thinks. What Kant ignores, in my opinion, and herein lies his fatal error, is the fact that the intellect always grows, however limited and closed in on itself. The intellect's field continually expands and this expansion is precisely synonymous with knowledge. In what does this expansion reside? To speak in a pseudo-Kantian way: in the emergence of new phenomena; of new categories. But I shall abandon the Kantian terminology going forward, because I consider it misleading. I shall say that the intellect's field expands through the emergence of new proper names and new grammatical rules of the language that the intellect is a part of. And from now on I shall call this expansion, knowledge.

The study of the Kantian categories provoked me, not biographically but methodologically, to identify the intellect with the field of languages. Last Friday Prof. L. Hegenberg[2] made a distinction between referent and logical words. Although I find this distinction somewhat problematic, I accept it for now, and I shall say that referent words correspond approximately to what Kant calls "impressions" ("*Wahrnehmungen*"), and logical words to what he calls categories. Today I shall deal only with the first type. But I shall substitute the nomenclature. I shall call referent words "names." Names are therefore, words that apparently refer to the external world. The external world is apparently called by proper names in order to be framed within the intellect's discourse. To call names is the intellect's first function. I shall distinguish between two types of names, which are, proper names and common names. This distinction is parallel to what Medieval Scholastics established between particulars and universals. Scholastics prove through the famous quarrel of universals that this distinction, far from being a problem of formal logic, is an epistemological problem, and from then on, an ontological and theological one. Allow me to clarify this problem a little.

Languages of the type spoken in Europe and the Near- and Middle-East, have a structure that allows for the classification of words from two different angles. They can be considered as words or as elements of phrases. The

2. Leonidas Hegenberg was a Professor at the Brazilian Institute of Philosophy and a close friend of Flusser's.

22

first criterion provides traditional grammatical terms such as substantive, adjective, verb etc. The second criterion provides terms such as subject, object, predicate etc. The first criterion involves problems such as declension, conjugation, etc. The second criterion involves problems such as the hierarchy of phrases. Transposing from grammar to logic, the first criterion involves the classic problems related to concepts, such as the problem of definition, generalization etc. The second criterion involves the classic problems related to judgment, such as the problem of deduction, induction, or rather, the problems of syllogisms, if we are to speak scholastically. Given the structure of this type of languages, discourse consists of phrases composed of words that obey rules. These rules have two levels: they regulate the form of the words within the phrase, and they regulate the form of the phrase within discourse. Transposing it to the terrain of logic, we may say that the intellect, or reason, informed by this type of languages consists of judgments composed of concepts that obey rules. These rules have two levels: they regulate the form of concepts within judgments, and they regulate the form of judgments within discursive thought. Since the existence of other types of language and intellect were largely being ignored during Antiquity and the Middle Ages, it was believed that this structure was the very structure of the human intellect "*tout court,*" and maybe even that of the Divine intellect. After all, men always imagine God in their own image.

The quarrel of the universals unfolds in the first level of meaning. We may roughly distinguish two positions: Realist and Nominalist.

Realist: universal names are the basic elements of the intellect, and as such, the basic elements of reality. They are, effectively, the Platonic ideas formalized. Particular names, or proper names, are existential applications of universal names. For example: "this is a horse." "This" is a proper name; "horse" is a universal name. My judgment affirms that "this" is a member of the class "horse." In respect to the judgment, the particular "this" is realized by being a member of the class "horse." The verb "is" affirms this fact. My judgment is knowledge, because it realized "this" in "horse;" because it realized the particular in the universal. I know because I universalize particulars. "*Universalia sunt ante res.*" Realism is the father of rationalism.

Nominalist: Universals emerge if I compare particulars. For example: "this and that are similar." I shall call this similarity "horse." Therefore, "this is a horse." The term "horse" is only the name that I gave to the similarity. It is a mere "*flatus vocis.*" The universal has no reality, since it emerges after the thing. "*Universalia sunt post res.*" My judgment is not knowledge because it adds nothing to the thing. The Franciscans, who are radical nominalists, do not admit, therefore, that reason can provide knowledge. Only unspoken faith can do it. Nominalism is the father of empiricism.

The quarrel of universals is a typical example of the projection of the structure of fusional languages onto the so-called "reality." It turns Latin grammar into the basis of ontology, metaphysics, and theology. It is trivial in the medieval meaning of the term, because it advances through the three paths of reading, writing, and recounting in the Latin language.

However, this quarrel must be faced, as trivial as it may be, because it speaks of the structure of our type of thought. After having been abandoned for four hundred years, it emerges again today. It is necessary to analyze how universals and particulars emerge in the intellect. Existentially speaking, the proper name emerges as a consequence of a gesture. It is the articulation of a gesture, such as, for example, "look there." That is why I have denominated the intellectual activity that produces particular names as "calling." Proper names are articulated gestures. This gesture has a "*Gestalt,*" or in other words, it points. The question "what does it point at?" is metaphysical and Kant has proven that it cannot be answered. Effectively, a formal analysis will prove that this question is either circular or meaningless. The gesture that points is the intellect's borderline situation. Furthermore: the gesture itself is already beyond the intellect. The gesture is not a reality but a virtuality. The proper name realizes this virtuality. By calling virtualities by name, the gesture realizes the intellect. *Mutatis mutandis,* by calling virtualities by name, the intellect realizes itself. Effectively: the proper name is the nucleus of reality. "World" and "Self," such metaphysical concepts, therefore false concepts, are nothing but the two horizons, and two aspects, of the proper name. The pointing aspect, the meaningful aspect, of the proper name, is its "world" aspect. And the articulating aspect, the symbolic aspect, of the proper name, is its "Self" aspect. It is precisely as the synthesis of these two aspects that the proper name is the nucleus, the germ, of reality.

Therefore: the proper name is a word of a particular language, for example of Portuguese or of symbolic mathematics. The virtualities that I very inappropriately called "world" and "Self," become realized within the field of particular languages. Languages are, as I said last week, sets of symbols and rules. "World" and "Self" become realized within these sets. I shall dedicate the next lecture to the discussion of how "world" and "Self" become realized within sets called fusional languages, that is, by predicating subjects, which are, in the final analysis, proper names and their derivatives. Today I shall draw your attention toward another fact. The Modern Age has gradually discovered phenomena that could be interpreted as gestures that point. I shall not discuss the reality of these discoveries, and that is why I call them phenomena, in a Kantian style. For example, the gesture of an amoeba that points toward light. The amoeba's heliotropism is, therefore, from our point of view, meaningful, since it points toward something. However, from the amoeba's point of view (if you allow me to express myself in this way), the gesture is meaningless, because it does not result in the articulation of a proper name that is an element of a ruled set. There is no amoebic language, or at least there is no amoebic language that can be recognized as such by our intellect. Consequently, we cannot translate ourselves into the amoebic point of view. We cannot converse with it. Consequently the amoeba does not exist for us, but is only one of these virtualities that has been realized by a proper name, in this case, "this is an amoeba."

The amoeba's quality of Being is what existential analysis calls "to be present-at-hand" (*Vorhandensein*). I shall give a second example: the inhabitant of the Andaman Islands. This native has gestures that are, from our point of view, meaningful, since they point toward something. These gestures are also meaningful from the Andamanese's point of view, because they are articulated. They result in something that we may call, through parallelism, "proper names," since they are symbols of a ruled set called "Andamanese language." Consequently I can, theoretically, equate the structure of this language to mine; I can translate myself to Andamanese and converse with him. The Andamanese exists with me; he is my "*Mitsein.*" And because the Andamanese realizes himself within a ruled set, not only can I know him (just like I can know the amoeba), but I can also recognize myself in him. When facing him I not only have knowledge (the result of the predication of subjects), but also recognition (the result of conversation). However, I shall verify, through this effort of translation toward conversation, that the structure through which the Andamanese realizes himself and the world is completely different from mine. Although the Andamanese exists, as I exist, he exists in a different form. And although the Andamanese realizes a world, as I do, he realizes an entirely different world. If I manage to converse with the Andamanese and to co-exist with him, I must, effectively, abandon my form of existence and the form of my world. There will never be an authentic conversation between the Andamanese and myself unless I change, or, vice versa, unless he changes. We are facing two different realities. For example: the two levels of meaning that characterizes my reality, the levels of concept and judgment, either cannot be found in the Andamanese language, or it has an entirely different form. My logic cannot be applied to Andamanese reality. If I apply my logic to Andamanese reality, I can only come to know it (as I know the amoebic reality), but I cannot come to recognize it. If I do this, I transform the Andamanese into something that is present-at-hand, and I deny him existential ontological dignity. And if I translate myself into Andamanese, I let go of my logic, and therefore cannot *know* him within my meaning of the term, although I could recognize him. Third example: all of you have gestures that point. These gestures result in proper names that are symbols of a ruled set called "Portuguese language." My gestures result in proper names that are symbols of a ruled set called "Czech language." Let us suppose that I cannot speak Portuguese. The structure of my language could be formalized into a ruled set called "symbolic logic," as well as yours. Your language and mine have an approximately identical structure, although they differ in several details. I can, therefore, in virtue of this similarity, translate myself into your reality without losing my structure. We can converse. We coexist. I can know you, and as I come to know you, I can recognize myself in you. To know and to recognize means that I can comprehend you. And you can, so I hope, comprehend me, including this argument. We coexist, because we speak the same type of language. We have the same form of Being and we exist within the same reality. Without a doubt, there are problems of translation between us, even if we all speak Portuguese, but these problems would disappear if we were to speak through mathematics or symbolic logic. This knowledge and recognition are the comprehension within conversation; they are the aim of the predicative realization of proper names, which is the intellect. And this is also the synthesis of what I would call "my theory of knowledge." With your permission, I shall elaborate this theory in my next lecture.

Bibliography:
Kant, I. *Critique of Pure Reason*, Introduction, from I to VII, but especially IV
Vossler, K. *Positivismus und Idealismus in der Sprachwissenschaft*
Whitehead, A.N. *Process and Reality*

III. Thought as Doubt

Last Friday I attempted to sketch, in a very rudimentary and therefore unsatisfactory manner, how proper names emerge in the intellect. Please note that, according to the epistemology that I am attempting to elaborate here before you, the proper name is anterior to the intellect and the external world. Effectively, the proper name is the ontic nucleus of both the intellect and the external world. According to the epistemology that I am elaborating for you, knowledge is ontologically anterior to knower and known. Knower and known are the two aspects and the two horizons of knowledge. Or, in order to reformulate this thought in more appropriate terms for this course of lectures: intellect and external world are the two aspects and the two horizons of language. The proper name as the source from which language springs, is therefore the source from which the intellect and the external world spring. I shall return several times to this problem during this course, because I shall seek to clarify it from an existential perspective and from a historical one. In the existential context, I shall seek to elaborate the climate that surrounds the emergence of the proper name, and I shall call this climate "poetic." In the historical context I shall seek to discuss some specific proper names that are the germs of that discourse called "Western history," and I shall call these proper names "myths." Poetry and myth surround, in a manner of speaking, the proper name at the moment of its irruption from nothingness, and it is necessary for me to at least mention this fact within this context. The proper name, as it irrupts, is an enigma in its plenitude. I apologize if this argument is not completely clear, because it presupposes a rationale, which I have not elaborated yet. I appeal to your intuition, and to your patience, as the argument should become clear during the course.

I repeat: the intellect and the external world are the two aspects of language. More precisely: the intellect is the structure of language and the external world is the meaning of language. The intellect is how phrases occur, and the external world is what the phrases mean. Phrases are processes, that is, they occur. While they occur, they realize intellects and external worlds. I shall dedicate this lecture to the discussion of how phrases occur. It will be, therefore, a discussion about the intellect. And I shall limit the discussion to phrases of languages of a particular type; of the fusional type. It will be, therefore, a discussion about the Western type of intellect. Since everyone in this room is an intellect of this type, we have at our disposal two avenues to access the proposed discussion: the extrospective and the introspective. We are able to observe how phrases occur within other intellects, and we can intuit how they occur. Therefore, this lecture will be limited to extrospective observation.

Note that I appeal to a vague term to denominate the occurrence that I shall discuss, that is, the term "phrase."

I do not say "thought," or "sentence," or "judgment," so as not to preconceive the argument. The term "phrase" evokes a form, a "*Gestalt,*" for example, a musical phrase, and this is the image that I wish to evoke in you. Let us consider therefore how these "*Gestalten*" occur. They occur through the activity of discourse. The course of phrases is, so to speak, inclined; it has a slope; it is a discourse. It runs, so to speak, downwards. What I am saying is not a poetic image, or a word game. (Although both poetic image and word game are justified when discussing language.) What I am describing is the attempt to visualize the process of the occurrence of phrases. Phrases originate at the summit of the proper name, and discourse toward the plain of the common name of all classes. They originate at the summit of the infinity of meaning, and they discourse toward zero meaning. The slope of the discourse is the measure of the exhaustion of meaning. In the course of the discourse, the infinite meaning of the proper name is progressively exhausted. The proper name has infinite meanings. Or, as traditional philosophy says, that which exists, has infinite attributes. The discourse progressively explicates the meanings implicit in the proper name, and the slope of the discourse is therefore, the explication of meanings. The course of the discourse is, at least in theory, infinite, since the number of meanings of a proper name is also infinite. I may eternally discourse around a proper name, and still, theoretically, I shall never explicate its meaning. We shall verify in the course of these lectures that in practice, that is, in history, there is a limit to the discourse, and an exhaustion of themes.

Discourse consists of phrases that predicate names. To predicate is synonymous with explicating meanings. The meaning of a name is explicated within the predicate. The phrase is the explication of a meaning because the phrase is a predicated name. As it is predicated, the name is transformed into the subject of a phrase. I shall leave the discussion of this transformation, which is effectively a leap between ontological layers, for another context. I shall define, for this context, the subject of a phrase as a group of words in which at least one is a name. The phrase is completed by a predicate. The predicate is a group of words in which at least one is a verb. I shall leave the discussion of verbs, which is effectively a discussion about forms of Being, for another context. Therefore, this is the standard form, the "*Gestalt*" of the phrase: "subject-predicate." This is obviously an extremely simplified form. The phrases that actually occur are generally much more complex. And there are, so to speak, defective phrases, such as "it rains" [*chove*] and "enough!" [*basta*!]. However, an analysis of phrases can, in theory, reduce every phrase to the simplified standard, or can complete defective phrases up to the simplified standard.

A phrase that consists of subject and predicate, for example the phrase "John loves," discourses from the subject "John" through the predicate "loves." A brief analysis of the verb "to love" allows a reformulation of this phrase to: "John is a lover." This phrase discourses from the subject "John," which is a proper name, toward the predicate "is a lover," which contains the name of a class. The phrase predicates the proper name "John" as it explicates one of its meanings, which is "being a lover." The common name that appears in the predicate as "lover," is a less meaningful name than the proper name "John," and this lesser meaning is the aim of the phrase. By predicating the proper name "John" in the common name "lover;" by affirming, therefore, that "John" is a member of the class "lover," our phrase is knowledge. Within the phrase, "John" becomes partially known as a member of a particular class. The full knowledge of "John" would be an argument that enumerates every class to which "John" belongs. As a proper name, "John" is a member of an infinity of classes. "John" cannot be exhaustively predicated. To reformulate: to predicate names, is to exhaust meanings through the enumeration of classes.

If you take into consideration, for just one moment, the Kantian problem of analytic and synthetic judgments, you will verify that the problem is overcome by my argument. Kant affirms that, "the grass is green," is an analytic judgment, because it predicates a class of which the name contained in the subject participates. Effectively, it says that the proper name "grass" is a member of the class "greenness." However, Kant affirms that the judgment "the green grass is in the garden" is a synthetic judgment, because it predicates something that is not contained in the name that is part of the subject. Kant is mistaken. To reformulate, the judgment says, strictly speaking: "This green grass is in the garden." And one of the meanings of the proper name "this green grass" is precisely that of being a member of the class "what is in the garden," and it is, therefore, an analytic judgment in the Kantian sense. Effectively, every phrase is an analytic judgment, if it is reduced to the proper name, which is the starting point of the slope of every phrase. However, this fact does not imply the impossibility of progressive knowledge, as Kant thinks, and the following argument will seek to demonstrate it.

Let us consider our standard phrase again: "John loves." It discourses; it is understandable; it is, therefore, part of the discourse. But it is as if something was missing in its form, as if its "*Gestalt*" was not complete. Our phrase discourses without an object, it is, therefore, as if the object was lost. Let us give an object to our phrase, and let us say, "John loves Mary." Let us try to reformulate this phrase, which is now composed of subject, predicate, and object: "John is a member of the class 'Mary's lovers.'" And let us hope, keeping in mind the happiness of both, that John is the sole member of this class. However, we may reformulate the phrase in a different manner: "Mary is a member of the class 'those who are loved by John.'" In this "*Gestalt*," which is more complete, the phrase establishes a relation between two proper names through the predicate. This relation has an active aspect, if seen from the subject, and a passive aspect, if seen from the object. We may invert this phrase, by saying that "Mary is loved by John," and we may, at last, give it the following form: "There is love from John for Mary." (Which would be an attempt to reconstruct the Greek aorist in Portuguese.) I leave the discussion of these formulations for when the analysis of the verb is our theme. In any case, we can say that the phrase synthesizes two proper names in the predicate: the two proper names that appear in both the subject and the object. Mary also becomes known in the predicate, like John, as "a loved one." And this is my argument against Kant. By synthesizing, in the predicate, the meanings of "John" and "Mary," our phrase is progressive knowledge, even though it is an analytic judgment in the Kantian sense.

The complete standard phrase, or, the phrase that has a *"Gestalt"* (subject: predicate: object), establishes a situation that I shall call from now on "a situation of reality." This is what Wittgenstein calls *"Sachverhalt"* and what Heidegger calls *"Bewandtnis."* "John loves Mary" establishes a relation between proper names; *"einen Verhalt von Sachen,"* and these proper names are explicated together in the predicate *"sind mit einander bewandt und zueinander gewendet."* The phrase "John loves Mary" realizes, in its predicate, a situation of reality, because in this predicate "John" is realized in his meaning as "the one who loves;" "Mary" in her meaning as "the one who is loved;" and then both these meanings are synthesized. As the realization of a situation, our phrase is, in this sense, a synthetic judgment, but this is not the Kantian meaning of the term. On the contrary, it is a dynamic meaning, which Kant ignores. The situation of reality established by our phrase is the synthetic result of a dialectic process that has the subject as thesis and the object as antithesis. And it is in this sense that the discourse is progressive, because it is predicative. It realizes situations of reality. There are therefore two progressive aspects of the discourse: it progresses as it exhausts the meanings of proper names toward common names. The unreachable aim of this progression is the common name of all classes, that is, the exhaustion of meaning. And it progresses by synthetically relating proper names into classes, and establishing situations of reality. The unreachable aim of this progression is to relate every proper name into a single class for all classes, therefore, a completely realized reality. As we can see, both aspects of the discourse's progress become confused at infinity, and are identical to a definitive silence. The aim of the discourse is, therefore, to end the enigma that proper names are. The aim of the discourse, that is, of the intellect, is absurd.

Let us reconsider, for a moment, the form of the phrase (subject: predicate: object). This is a specific form, which has been rigorously studied through existential analysis. This form is called "project." The phrases of fusional languages are projected situations of reality. The total sum of these situations, therefore the external world, in which the intellect exists (if we appeal to existentialist terminology), is a projected reality. In the standard phrase the predicate projects the subject toward the object. The phrase flows through a jet called "predicate," from a substratum called "subject," toward an obstacle called "object," and in this jet it realizes a project called "a situation of reality." Thus, this particular form of project characterizes the external world that languages of our type establish. The so-called eternal problems of philosophy are the result of this structure of our world. It is possible to analyze the phrase from the subject, object, or predicate, and these analyses will result in different "*Weltanschauungen;*" different worldviews. And I insist in the affirmative that, at this stage, the concept of a grammatical analysis of the phrase as synonymous with the ontological analysis of reality must have started to acquire a degree of plausibility for you.

If I analyze the phrase from the perspective of the subject, the phrase presents itself as a form, in which something is being transferred from the subject toward an object. Let us call this something "quality," and let us call subject and object "substances," thus, we shall have the main guidelines of the Aristotelian worldview. The view of the world, as an ordered transfer of qualities from substance to substance, is the result of viewing the world from the subject of the phrase, which established a situation of reality. If I analyze the phrase from the perspective of the object, I shall have a view of the situation as consisting of the impact of something that projected itself upon the object. This view corresponds approximately to the mechanistic worldview, which is the fundament for the science of the 17th to the 19th centuries: the world as a chain of situations, that is, as a chain of forces that act upon bodies. From this, let us say, "objective" point of view, the fundamental structure of reality is inertia, since the object represents the passive side of the phrase. If I analyze the phrase from the perspective of the predicate, the phrase presents itself as a process at whose extremes lie the subject and the object, like horizons, but whose real nucleus is predication. This worldview could be characterized by the term "Heraclitean river," it is also the ground for the Hegelian worldview and is fundamental to contemporary science: the world presents itself as a chain of becoming; the world is not, but turns into, becomes, happens. The highest expression of this worldview is Nietzsche; the world as will to power, and that which wills is the subject of the situation, and power is its object, but the situation's reality is in the willing, which is the predicate. The world as a collection of fields, in which energy reaches power in the form of matter, is the scientific consequence of Nietzschean philosophy. All of these worldviews are the result of the form of the phrase in our languages. We may oscillate between these worldviews, or we may seek a synthesis of these worldviews, but we may not conceive of the world through a different structure. We cannot do it, because the structure of the external world is precisely the structure of our intellect, and the structure of our intellect is the structure of our languages. I believe that this is exactly what the Kantian critique of pure reason establishes. Our world has, categorically, the structure of our languages. Our world is the realization of a project contained within our languages, and our mind is the obverse of this realization of the world. With this argument, I believe to have overcome the nefarious dichotomy intellect/thing, or subject/object, which adheres to classical epistemology and ontology like a plague. If knowledge is defined as the adequation of intellect to thing, then we do not need any divine help for this adequation, as Descartes thinks; nor do we need to despair in relation to this adequation, as the skeptical rationalists and empiricists think. Intellect and thing are adequated through language. That is why progressive knowledge is perfectly possible, and the sciences prove it. It is true that this knowledge is purely linguistic, that it consists of chains of phrases that discourse, but this does not diminish the epistemological value of that discourse. The thing-in-itself, that which is therefore beyond language, is ineffable. If it is something, then it is the meaning of the proper names in its fullness, and language realizes this meaning as it discourses about proper names through their predication. This is knowledge, and all the rest is inarticulate metaphysics.

For methodological reasons I cannot delve, within the current context, into any considerations of the concept of "project." However, it must be obvious, even in the current context, that the project, which has been established by the structure of our languages, establishes a limitation to our intellect. This is what Wittgenstein means when he says that the history of thought is a collection of progressive wounds, which the intellect acquires as it throws itself against its iron bars. And it is also what Rilke means as he says, in his poem, characteristically called *The Panther*: "*und hinter tausend Stäben keine Welt*" (and behind a thousand iron bars, no world). However, the project of our languages not only limits our intellect, it also makes the intellect expandable. The limitations are always present, enclosing the intellect. But these limitations always crumble against the intellect's attack. The intellect expands not only through the continuous emergence of proper names, but also through the emergence of new rules, and through the disappearance of old rules. I shall have opportunity during this lecture to discuss both these aspects of the intellect's expansion. What I intend to do at this moment with these considerations, is to offer you a definition of the term "intellect," with which I am operating.

I shall define intellect as the field in which phrases occur. A field, as physics applies the meaning of the term, is the structure of occurrences. A magnetic field, for example, is the more or less imaginary lines along which iron filings would manifest around a magnetic pole. This is the meaning with which I wish to endow the term "field," according to the definition that I am proposing. The intellect is a particular structure in which phrases occur, if and when, they occur. This is an almost Kantian image of the intellect (or as he would say, of pure reason). It overcomes the empiricists' *tabula rasa*, as well as the rationalists' knowledge factory. But the image is hardly Kantian. It differs from Kant because it admits the existence of intellects with different structures, and it differs further because it admits that the structures of the intellect are progressively malleable. Should you accept my definition, it will condemn you, as it condemns me, to a relativist approach in relation to the validity of all knowledge. Any given knowledge is valid only within an intellect's given structure. I say this in relation to the arguments that constitute knowledge. For now, I remain silent in relation to the notion of truth. We shall see during this course that the term "truth" varies according to historical context, and that the appropriate place for us to discuss truth will be the field of poetry. I repeat, therefore, that the definition of intellect as a field, in which phrases of a given language occur, condemns not only the truth of these phrases, but also their validity, to relativism. I do not believe, however, that this relativism necessarily has the flavor of despair.

An obvious objection to my definition would be to say that phrases from different languages can occur within the same intellect. I ask you not to formulate this objection, because this will be the theme of my next lecture. I believe to have made it clear that the problem of polyglotism is an epistemological and ontological problem of the first degree. The translation of phrases from one language to another, and the translation of intellects from one language to another, thus becomes the very same test for the theory of knowledge that I am endeavoring to develop here with you. I shall, therefore, deal with translation, before dealing with conversation in a proper sense.

Allow me to recapitulate, in a few words, what I have sought to elaborate in this lecture. Proper names are the source of language. From these proper names, predicates are projected, and in this process proper names transform into the subjects of phrases. Predicates that are projected from proper names contain verbs that are articulations of the modalities of Being, of proper names. The aim of predication is the common name. The progressive enumeration of these common names is the slope of the discourse, which consist of phrases. In this process, other proper names may be included in the phrases as objects. The predicate establishes situations of reality in this type of phrase. The external world is a collection of these situations of reality, and is, in this sense, the meaning of discourse. The intellect is the field of discourse. External world and intellect are two aspects of discourse.

Before we end this lecture, I wish to say one more thing: discourse is not uniform. It divides into several branches, called "arguments," and these arguments discourse on different planes of meaning. This division of the discourse into arguments – of which, one example could be physics, and another, could be art critique – arrests, so to speak, the speed of the discourse. Arguments can stagnate, or they can exhaust themselves. This stagnation relates to the predication of common names toward other common names. This problem will be the theme of a future lecture. On the other side, the slope of the discourse is not uniform. It has contrary movements, which are called reflexive. These movements of thought predicate toward the proper names from the common name. These reflexive movements, roughly called "philosophy," will also be considered later. I give you these provisos in order to delineate the terrain of the discussion that will follow this lecture.

Bibliography:
Cassirer, E. *Substanzbegriff und Funktionsbegriff*
Rickert, H. *Die Logik des Praedikats und das Problem der Ontologie*

IV. The Multiplicity of Languages

This course has been forced toward a digression due to the arguments that have been formulated in relation to the theory of knowledge. Therefore, I shall dedicate this "lecture" to this digression. It is becoming obvious that the test of our theory of knowledge will be a yet to be formulated theory of translation. This theory should explicate two opposing facts: it should explain why translations are possible, by giving a special meaning to the term "translation," and it should explain why translations are impossible, by giving a different meaning to the same term. Last Friday, Prof. Hegenberg gave an example of the first case: it is possible to translate from two-dimensional geometry to three-dimensional geometry. I can now give an example of the second case: it is impossible to translate from two-dimensional geometry to the language of mysticism. If we are to give credit to traditional philosophy, including the neopositivists, then the three languages being discussed: two-dimensional geometry, three-dimensional geometry, and mysticism, all mean "something," that is, "reality." The phrases of both geometries as well as the phrases of mysticism are true, according to this philosophy, if and when they mirror a situation of reality. However, I shall seek to prove, that the phrases of two-dimensional geometry are impossible to translate into the phrases of mysticism. In one-way or another: Either (1) the language of geometry is meaningful and the language of mysticism is not, or the language of mysticism is meaningful and the language of geometry is not, or even, they are both meaningless. Or (2) both languages are meaningful, but the impossibility of translation between them proves that their meaning does not reside in a mirroring of "something" that is common to both. It is obvious that we cannot condemn one of these languages, or both, to a lack of meaning. It is, therefore, the second alternative that must be explained by a theory of translation, which we shall seek to elaborate today. A preliminary consideration becomes desirable: the illustrations that I have provided exemplify the type that I shall call the layers of language. Two-dimensional and three-dimensional geometry, as well as mysticism, are layers of a "natural" language, for example, of Portuguese. I shall call translations between layers "vertical translations." There are natural languages such as Portuguese and Swahili. We can imagine translation of a mystical phrase from Portuguese to Swahili. I shall call this type of translation "horizontal translation." I shall consider the "natural" languages as the starting point for this argument, without examining, in the present context, their problematic "naturalness."

I shall discuss only the languages of the fusional type, and I shall consider the possibility of translation between languages of a different structure at a later date. To radically simplify, fusional languages are characterized by the following structure: They consist of words. These words allow themselves to be considered within or without

46

phrases. When considered from without the phrase, these words allow inflection. I shall consider only two types of inflection: declension and conjugation. Declension is the inflection of words of the type "substantive," or similar words. Conjugation is the inflection of words of the type "verb." There are inflections that transform words of one type into another. These, I may consider later. Declension is responsible for that aspect of our external world that we call "space," and conjugation for that aspect that we call "time." Languages of another structure cannot result in worlds that have aspects of space and time within our meaning of these terms.

Words can also be considered within the context of the phrase. From this point of view, the problems of subject, predicate, object etc., and the problems of indication, interrogation, imperative etc., will emerge, which I shall consider later if I have time.

Languages of our type present themselves, if seen from without, in two ways: as sounds and as drawings. (Spoken and written language.) A brief consideration of the drawings will reveal that they are symbols of sounds, with a few exceptions, for example, numbers. However, systems of symbols that do not symbolize the sounds of spoken language, such as for example, symbolic logic or musical notation, have been developed in the course of the discourse. The systems of symbols that represent the sounds of spoken language (the alphabets) are the result of the effort to translate the meaning of spoken language onto the two dimensions of the plane. The systems of symbols that do not represent the sounds of spoken language are the result of the effort to translate the structure of spoken language onto the two dimensions of the plane. Spoken language serves as the referential system for all of these systems; hence, they are all derived. These efforts of translation are crowned by considerable, albeit limited, success. The alphabets translate the meaning of spoken language, but not every meaning. Mathematics and musical notation translate the structure of spoken language, but not every structure. This is a problem that we will deal with, in detail, in the future. It would be a mistake to call the symbols of mathematics or logic "ideograms." The ideograms of the written languages of the East are independent from spoken language; for example, they have far greater autonomy than algebraic symbols. It is possible that, historically, some ideograms emerged through an effort to translate spoken language. Others emerged from a pictorial effort, that is, from an inarticulate gesture. However, the writing system of the East is an autonomous whole; and "structurally" it is entirely different from our type of languages.

This is, therefore, the structure of our languages, albeit radically simplified. My theory of translation affirms that, given such fundamental structural identity, translations are possible between languages of our type. According to my theory, translation consists of the adequation of a phrase, let us say a Portuguese one, to another phrase, let us say an Arab one, in the following manner: First we analyze the Portuguese phrase, both at the phrase-level, and at the word-level. Afterwards we shall choose Arab phrases of a similar structure, and Arab words of a similar type. The result, which will be an Arab phrase that consists of Arab words, we shall call "the translation of a

Portuguese phrase." It is obvious that the new phrase will not be perfectly equivalent to the original one, since there will not be a point-by-point correspondence. The situation of reality that the Arab phrase will establish will not be identical to the situation of reality established by the Portuguese phrase. Both realities will be different, and in this sense I can say that translation is impossible. But they will be structurally similar, and in this sense I can say that translation is possible. Let us consider, for a moment, why both situations of reality will be different.

I shall give two examples. First example: The conjugation of the Indo-Germanic verb realizes time by articulating it in the past, present, and future. The conjugation of the Semitic verb realizes time by articulating it in the past and future. In the Semitic reality, the present is not time. If I translate the Portuguese phrase "*eu falo*," [I speak] to the Hebrew phrase "*ani omer*," the situation of reality will have been entirely changed. The situation of "*eu falo*" is dynamic because it involves time. The situation of "*ani omer*" (literally "I speaker") is static, because it does not involve time. However, this is, nonetheless, a translation, because the structure of the Portuguese phrase is "*eu sou falador*" [I am a speaker], which approximately corresponds to the structure of the Hebrew phrase – a language that does not have the verb "to be," and, therefore, does not allow the translation of the Portuguese word "*sou*" [I am]. Second example: Consider the following group of words "*a casa do livro*" [the book's house]. Due to declension, this group establishes a relation between two names, which is the nucleus of a situation of reality. "*A casa*" [house] is nominative, "*do livro*" [the book's] is genitive, and a relation of the type "property" therefore characterizes the situation. The house is a property of the book. It implies the situation "the book has a house." Consider now a translation to Hebrew "*bejt hasefer.*" What is being declined now is the first name "*bejt*" (house). Our "nominative" and "genitive" categories are not applicable to the situation of reality that is emerging. Nevertheless, this is an approximately legitimate translation, due to our analysis, which resulted in "the book has a house." It is true that Hebrew does not know verbs like "to have" and "to be" and does not know the present. Therefore, the phrase "the book has a house" is untranslatable. However, Hebrew has a dative that is very similar to ours. I can, thus, construct the Hebrew phrase "*Bajit lisefer*" (literally "house to book") and I can, very laboriously, adequate the Portuguese verb "*ter*" [to have] to this dative, for example, "the house belongs to the book." I can affirm, therefore, that the translation of "the book's house" to "*bejt hasefer*" is approximately correct. But I shall have a surprise. "*Bejt hasefer,*" which I have now so laboriously discovered to be "the book's house" means "*escola*" [school]. And this discovery of mine will be fatidic to my belief in a situation of reality beyond languages. There is no school as such, which both languages seek to articulate, and our example proves it existentially. The most we can say is the following: within the context of the world created by the Hebrew language the words "*bejt hasefer*" occupy an approximately corresponding place to the one occupied by the word "*escola*" (that is, a place of contemplation and *otium*, "*scholé*"), within the context of the world created by the Portuguese language.

Everything I have just said refers to that type of translation that I called "horizontal" in the introduction to the problem. The phrases that we have considered until now participate, approximately, on the same linguistic layer, which I have denominated by the term "conversation," and this will be from now on, a technical term. I shall now define the layer of arguments that converse verses. I shall define "verse" as a phrase that predicates an original proper name, and I shall define the linguistic layer, in which verses occur, as "poetry." These are definitions formulated "ad hoc," and I ask that you accept them, therefore, without comprehending the ends to which I appeal to these terms. Everything that we have discussed up until now refers to the translation of Portuguese conversational phrases to Hebrew conversational phrases, therefore, to horizontal translation. Thus, I shall formulate my theory of this type of translation as follows: Horizontal translations are mutual adequations between two structures of languages from corresponding layers. Translations will be more successful according to how similar the structures are, and according to how lacking in meaning they are. I believe that my definition is now plausible in relation to the similarity of structures. Now I shall deal with the poverty of meaning.

In previous expositions, I defined discourse as the progressive exhaustion of meaning through the predication of names. The process starts through the predication of proper names, whose meaning is infinite. Proper names appear in the discourse through an activity I have denominated as "to call," but now I am going to change this term. I shall say that this activity of calling is the activity of poetry. Phrases that predicate new proper names produced by poetry are verses. Verses constitute the poetic layer of language. The conversational layer is the result of an effort of vertical translation: it consists of verses translated into prose. Through this translation, proper names are translated into common names, and the dense and implicit structure of the verse is loosened and explicated. It is obvious that this is a progressive translation. The poetic quality of the verse is progressively prosified by the conversation in course. The conversational layer of language may, therefore, be stratified into sublayers according to the degree of prosification reached. The sub-layer, from which our examples of horizontal translation were extracted, is relatively underdeveloped. It is placed relatively close to the layer of poetry. This is the reason for the relative difficulty of translating from Portuguese to Hebrew within this sub-layer. If the examples had been taken from a more developed and more prosaic layer, for example from that conversation called "chemistry," the difficulties in translation would have been much smaller. I imagine that the translation of the Portuguese phrase "*uma molécula de sal de cozinha consiste de um átomo de sódio e outro de cloro*" [one molecule of table salt consists of one atom of sodium and another of chloride] would not have been so difficult. At a more advanced layer, for example the layer of phrases such as "Na + Cl = NaCl" the difficulty in translation would be minimal, and would consist only in the substitution of the Latin alphabet by the Hebrew one. Finally, we would have arrived at the purely formal layer of symbolic logic, and there would not be any difficulty in translation, because any translation would disappear on this layer. Formal logic is the articulation of the common structure of Portuguese and Hebrew, and on this layer, which is exempt of meaning, both languages are confused with each other. If analyzed, horizontal translation would reveal itself as a complicated case of successive vertical translations. The Portuguese phrase to be translated to Hebrew is translated vertically to the layer of symbolic logic, and retranslated from there to the corresponding Hebrew conversational layer. The speed with which we execute translations, in practice, conceals and veils the complexity of this process. In the vertical translation to a formal layer, we progressively strip the phrase of its meaning and explicate its structure. In the retranslation to the conversational layer, we cover the phrase again with meaning, but a meaning that is obviously slightly different from the first. Very prosaic phrases, that is, relatively poor in meaning and closer to the formal layer, are easily translated, because the path to be followed is relatively direct. Phrases that are full of meaning, such as verses, are untranslatable, even between languages with very similar structures, because the path is too long. This is the fact, which my definition of horizontal translation articulates.

Before considering vertical translations, I want to answer an objection formulated by our young friend,[3] that is, the one that had the translatability of Portuguese to Andamanese as a theme. If my argumentation is valid, it is obvious that we can translate from Portuguese to Andamanese as long as we find a formal fundament common to both languages. I shall disconsider the fact that, even

<hr />

3. Someone in the audience who is not mentioned by name.

if this common fundament is found, the translation will be very vague, given that, for example, declension and conjugation do not exist in the Andamanese language, and that therefore, neither space nor time exist in Andamanese, according to our meaning of these terms. However, here is a purely formal aspect of the problem: in our symbolic logic, if $a = b$ is true, then $a \neq b$ is not true. But I know, from my knowledge of Andamanese, that a dancer can simultaneously be a sweet potato, and not be one. The structure of this language must be, therefore, entirely different from mine. Even so, should I discover some common fundament, it would probably be so tenuous that it would make any translation effort laughable and frustrating. I am not saying that these translations are impossible, but they must deviate from the original in an absurd way. I know that Lin Yu Tang had fits of laughter when presented with translations of Li Tai Po done by Ezra Pound, and it is this comic nature of the effort that I have in mind.

Now I shall quickly consider vertical translation, of which, horizontal translation is nothing but a complex case. I borrow the example provided by Prof. Hegenberg last Friday. I translate vertically from three-dimensional geometry to two-dimensional geometry. The structure of the language of three-dimensional geometry contains, among other logic and formal elements, three Cartesian axes that coordinate points: these three axes are prosified space and derive, in a last analysis, from the declension of names. The language of three-dimensional geometry is a highly prosaic conversation distanced from poetry. I shall attempt to prosify this language even further, and I shall eliminate the axes. I shall impoverish the language of geometry with this elimination, because from now on, all the points of which I speak will have only two coordinates, and all of my equations will be square and have only two roots. My new language will be more economical and simpler, and will employ fewer terms. It will not be any less vast than three-dimensional geometry, because the whole of three-dimensional geometry can be projected upon two-dimensional geometry. But it will be less meaningful. The names that I shall employ will be one step further away from the proper names that are predicated in verses. As it is one step further from the fullness of the real situation established by the verse, two-dimensional geometry has, in this sense, less reality than three-dimensional geometry, and, in this sense, three-dimensional space is more real than two-dimensional space. This is, therefore, why I translate vertically: in order to reach a greater economy of terms and less reality. In the end, vertical translation is nothing but a general aspect of the predication of proper names toward common names. Effectively: the language of two-dimensional geometry is, as a whole, a class to which three-dimensional geometry belongs. I shall define, therefore, vertical translation as follows: ascending vertical translation is to vert[4] the verse toward conversation, and to progressively convert

4. In Portuguese Flusser uses the verb *verter* from the Latin *vertere*, which means to turn, or to flip something. According to the OED the verb "to vert" has exactly the same meaning and etymology and is the root of "to invert," "to convert," "to pervert," "to revert" etc. So even though it is no longer in common use, I chose to use "to vert" throughout the text in order to retain Flusser's play with the words that are based on this root. [TN]

the verse into prose. Descending vertical translation is the attempt to revert the conversation toward the verse and is, therefore, an inverted translation. I shall return to the problem of vertical translation when I discuss verse and poetry.

Let us now consider the attempt to translate a phrase from two-dimensional geometry to the language of mysticism. I said that our type of languages could be considered as systems of words organized into phrases, and that these phrases can be classified, for example, as indicative, imperative, interrogative etc. The verse, in its dense structure, is a synthesis of these diverse forms of phrases. Conversation explicates this dense structure into the forms enumerated above. Two-dimensional geometry verts the verse toward indicative and interrogative forms of phrases by vertical translation. Mysticism, if formally analyzed, will be revealed as a conversation that verts the verse toward imperative and interrogative forms of phrases by vertical translation. These are, therefore, two vertical translations of verses that point toward two different horizons of language. The desire to translate two-dimensional geometry to mysticism or vice-versa is, therefore, the wish to encompass two different horizons of language. This encompassing cannot be done by the adequation of both structures, and in this sense, translation is not possible. It is possible to adequate geometry to mysticism, but this must be done through a concentric translation that points to the verse from which both conversations originate; therefore, through a kind of vertically descending and concentric translation. This type of convergent translation, whose inverted discourse predicates common names toward the proper name contained in the verse, is called "philosophy." As an inverted and reflexive discourse, philosophy seeks to translate every layer of conversation upon itself through its reversion toward the verse. Philosophy can, through this encompassing movement, englobe mysticism and two-dimensional geometry in the form of phrases that predicate common names toward proper names contained in verses. This is philosophy's role as a critique of language.

Therefore I reformulate: Horizontal translation is the mutual adequation between two corresponding layers, of the structures of two languages. And a translation will be all the more successful depending on how similar both structures are, and of how poor in meaning each layer is. Horizontal translation is a complex of vertically ascending and descending translations. Ascending vertical translation is the verting of the verse toward conversation, which progressively converts the verse into prose. Descending vertical translation is the attempt to revert the conversation toward the verse. The sum of ascending translations is the discourse's progress. The sum of descending translations is philosophy.

What have I achieved with this theory that I am presenting to you? I have eliminated the pseudo concept of an extra linguistic reality from our future argumentation. I do not translate a Portuguese phrase to a Hebrew one because both refer to the same extra linguistic situation, but because the structures of both languages have similarities. I have eliminated the Wittgensteinian "*Sachverhalt.*" As a secondary product of my theory I have managed a plausible explication of the translation process and perhaps the germ for a more adequate translation technique. I have managed to encompass, through my theory of translation, both the progressive aspect and the reflexive aspect of the intellect as the field of languages. And I have managed to formally define this intellectual movement called "philosophy."

What have I not achieved with my theory? I have not managed to explicate why there are languages of similar, and of different structures. I have not managed to explicate how translations from spoken to written language are done. I have not managed to explicate the relation between strictly spoken language, and those other languages such as music, dance etc. And I have not managed to explicate a series of other problems that you will certainly and mercifully point out. However, I still believe that I have made some progress all the same. I have cleared the ground for a future discussion of the consequences of the epistemology that we are discussing. In this sense, this lecture was not discourse but excourse, for which I apologize, given my extreme didactic inability.

This time I do not offer a bibliography because the theory exposed is my own.

V. Translation as Knowledge

Let us consider the problem of translation once more, but only in order to clarify a different problem from the ones that have preoccupied us up until now. My constant preoccupation was to challenge, in you, the common sense that affirms the existence of a world external to language, and to eliminate the very term "external world" from a disciplined philosophical discussion. Today, my intention is to consider, with you, the meaning of the term "Self," therefore, that nucleus from which we philosophize. But first, allow me some preliminary observations.

The fundamental difference between Western philosophy and that mental discipline that can be called "Indian philosophy" (by way of parallelism), resides in its starting point. Western thinkers start from the "Self" and doubt the "external world" in order to investigate it. Indian thinkers start from the "world" and doubt the "Self" in order to investigate it, and are, from our point of view, inverted empiricists. That is why Western thought tends toward Idealism, that is, toward a worldview in which the "Self" is totally different from the "world," and in which the "world" is an inferior ontological consequence of the "Self." The Indians, in turn, tend toward the kind of materialism that we call "spiritualism" in the West. This is a worldview in which the "Self" is an appearance of the "external world;" in which there is no ontological difference between "world" and "Self," and in which, therefore, spirits can materialize. In Western thought, it is perfectly conceivable to doubt everything except the "Self": to doubt the "Self" is something that is difficult to conceive. In India, it is precisely this doubt of the "Self" that propels thought, and the Buddhist belief in the illusory nature of the "Self" is a logical consequence of this inverted investigation. Western thought, as a doubting of the external world, results in natural science, which is a type of progressive knowledge of the external world through disciplined doubt. Indian thought, because it is a doubting of the Self, results in meditation, which is a type of progressive knowledge of the Self through disciplined doubt. Western natural science results in technology, which is the manipulation and domination of the external world. Meditation results in the manipulation and domination of the Self. Existential thought is one of the few Western attempts to follow the movement of Indian thought, although, accidentally so. It is not surprising that Heidegger is more widely read in Japan than in Germany.

I shall begin with a quick analysis of the "Self" through Existentialism. When I find myself, I always find myself within a situation, that is, I am in the world. The form that my Self has is always a being here (*Dasein*). In this being here of mine, my situation preoccupies me, because it encloses me. The things, of which my situation consists, oppose themselves to me and bar my project. Things determine who I am. As I project myself against things, I verify that they may be apprehended, comprehended, and undertaken [*empreendidas*] (to appeal to a term from Prof. Amora), and that I may free myself as I transform them into instruments. However, why am I able to do this? I am able to do this because my form of being is different from that of things. Things stand in front of me; they are full of themselves. They are, in Sartre's words, "*trop choses*" (excessively "things").[5] But I have a vacuity inside me; I am invaded by nothingness. I am a defective form of being, because I am here for death. Because of this defect of mine, I feel nausea for things that are overly full. Things bore me. And my nausea is the starting point of my decision to free myself of things. My vacuity, which is my being here for death, allows me to transcend things. It is because of this vacuity that I extend my hands to reach things. It is because of this vacuity that I exist. To exist means to be invaded by nothingness. This nothingness within me, which is the very fundament of my being here, is a crack in the compacted situation in which I find myself. It is in virtue of this clear night of the anguish of nothingness that I discover within me that I see things as they are; that they are things and not nothingness. The nothingness within me, the nothingness that I am, is the crack through which the world emerges in order

5. In the original version Flusser renders this phrase in French without the preposition "de," which is explained by the phrase in Portuguese in brackets. He is obviously paraphrasing Sartre and he is not speaking about "lots of things," which would demand the preposition in the French phrase, but that things are too full of themselves; too real. Perhaps his formulation is not good French form, but by inserting the preposition, it would point to a different meaning. So I have chosen to keep Flusser's original form in French and to let it pass as "poetic license." [TN]

to establish itself around me as the situation, in which, I find myself. The situation around me, my circumstance, sprung from the nothingness that hides within my core. It was the nothingness within me that established the world. As you can see, this ontological analysis of "*Dasein*" ends up as a kind of Buddhism, although in a kind of Western Buddhism. The nothingness within me, of which the existentialists speak, is an active nothingness, it is "nullifying," and bears little semblance to *Nirvana*, of which it is a parallel. Effectively, this nothingness is the place left vacant by the God of Christianity, after He was killed, in Nietzsche's words. Existentialism is Christianity inverted.

This whole preamble serves as an introduction to the consideration of translation that I propose. Let us introspectively consider what happens when I translate, for example, the Portuguese phrase "*João ama Maria*" to the English phrase "John loves Mary." At the beginning of the process I have a thought: "*João ama Maria.*" But what is my intention when I say, "I have a thought"? Let us attempt to answer this difficult question. The thought "*João ama Maria*" occurs in a space called the "Self." I am able to visualize this space as a computer (for example, a brain), and I can say that the thought "*João ama Maria*" occurs in this computer called the "Self," and that is why I say that I have this thought. However, to affirm that I have this thought, "*João ama Maria*", is, in turn, also a thought. This second thought cannot occur in the same computer, or brain, as the first thought, because it encompasses the first thought and all other thoughts of the same level. There must be a computer that is the computer of all computers. In other words: the thought "I have a thought – '*João ama Maria*' occurs at a different level from that of '*João ama Maria.*'" Obviously, I could therefore construct an argument that would be a reduction of the "Self" *ad infinitum*. But I could try to save the "Self" and say that all of these infinite levels are part of the same computer, of the same brain, and that this computer is a place of infinite levels. But this type of place will be exactly what German philosophy calls "*Bodenlos*"; it will be groundless. Any attempt to localize the "Self," be it naive (for example, in the human brain as the behaviorists do, or in the pineal gland as Descartes does), or be it sophisticated (for example, in the psyche or in the soul), is an attempt doomed to end in frustration and failure.

Let us try another answer to our question: What do I mean when I say I have the thought, "*João ama Maria*"? The phrase "*João ama Maria*" occurs within a general process called "conversation," that is: it does not occur in isolation. Conversation is a fabric of phrases united by links called "arguments." It is a fluid fabric that is in continuous and progressive expansion. At certain places (it might be better to say "moments") of this fabric, the threads of the argument crisscross, regroup, and reformulate. These moments of the process of conversation are the knots of its fabric. Conversation consists of these knots united by arguments. Conversation is the field in which thoughts linked by arguments that crisscross occur. On previous Fridays I have called this field "intellect." Conversation is the intellect's field, in which thoughts crisscross. Today I shall call these crossing points, "Selves." I shall define conversation as the intellect's field, in which thoughts (phrases) occur, constantly regrouped and re-formulated by "Selves." Conversation is a field of Selves that converse. Selves are an aspect of conversation, that is: Selves are how the conversation processes itself. That is how we should interpret Heidegger's phrase: "We, human beings, are a conversation" [*Gespräch*], and that is how we could attempt to define the term "Self." If I say, "I have a thought – '*João ama Maria*,'" I intend to say that this thought occurs in a particular way called "Self." My analysis of the term "Self" is not complete, because I started from the layer of language I called conversation, and not from that other I called poetry. On that other layer, we shall verify later, that "Selves" are moments when language finds itself open to nothingness, in order to inhale it. However, for my current purpose, my analysis is sufficient. So I shall proceed with it.

The phrase "*João ama Maria*" is part of a Portuguese conversation. I have this phrase because I am how Portuguese phrases occur. I am, effectively, a knot of Portuguese phrases, and a conduit for Portuguese phrases; and this is the only intellectually satisfactory meaning of the term "Self." I repeat, therefore, the problem that preoccupies us: what happens when I translate the Portuguese phrase to "John loves Mary"? I sought to show, in the last exposition, the formal aspect of the problem. I sought to show that the apparently horizontal translation is, in reality, a series of complex vertical translations. I do not translate "*João*" as "John," "*ama*" as "loves," and "*Maria*" as "Mary," as a superficial observation of the translation might suggest. I neither consult a "*Sachverhalt*," that is, I do not appeal to João and Maria to then reformulate their amorous relation in an English manner, as a philosophy that believes in an extra linguistic reality would demand. But I translate, "*João ama Maria*," to a formal level of the Portuguese language, for example, "ArB." This formal level is also valid for the English language (at least in a general sense), and, by applying a Portuguese-English dictionary, I substitute the symbols for the terms "John," "loves," and "Mary." I establish, effectively, an uninterrupted chain of phrases that joins "*João ama Maria*" to "John loves Mary," and the leap between the two phrases, the "*Übersetzung*," is an illusion created by the speed with which I run through the intermediary stages between both languages.

However, an existential analysis of the phenomenon of translation will not agree with the formal analysis that I have just sketched, and this discrepancy demands closer attention. When I have the thought "*João ama Maria*," I am integrated within a situation of reality. I am really myself. The reality, in which I am integrated, is the Portuguese conversation. Everything around me is meaningful, in the sense that it points to something. For example: "*João ama Maria*" is a meaningful part of my circumstance, and is a part of reality. I am real; I am really myself because I have thoughts of the type "*João ama Maria.*" To say that I am really myself or that I am really here is to say that I am integrated in the Portuguese conversation. "Reality" and "integration in the conversation" are either synonyms, or mere noise. When I start to translate, it is as if the real ground beneath my feet begins to dissolve. My being-here becomes problematized. The Self that I am, that Self that has thoughts, threatens to disintegrate as these thoughts

65

start to become formalized and symbolized. This is a kind of progressive and disciplined alienation. When I finally reach the stage of translation that corresponds to phrases such as ArB, it becomes very difficult to say that I am the one who has this thought. This thought is so formal, and so lacking in meaning, that it becomes completely impersonal and has nothing of mine. It is almost as if the Self had evaporated through the verticality of the argument. If I now proceed to reendow it with meaning, if I cover it with flesh and skin again, it is as if a Self had materialized around the thought. When the thought, "John loves Mary" emerges, I can, once again, say that I am the one who has this thought. But now this Self that has the English thought is part of the English conversation. This Self is a different existence from the one that had the thought "*João ama Maria*" because it is thrown into a different situation. Its reality is another. However, in a certain way, the English Self is identical to the Portuguese Self, because they are linked through vertical translation, which is a chain of uninterrupted links. I may, therefore, widen my definition of the term "Self," by saying that I am that knot in the conversation through which several languages of a common fundament can be linked. It is through the Selves that the different conversations are interlinked. The polyglot Selves guarantee the unicity, although problematically, between languages that are different, but of uniform structural substratum.

The problem that I have just summarily exposed is of great existential importance. However, it does not seem to have been fully appreciated until now. It is obvious that every translator intimately experiences this problem. There is a famous saying that says we live as many times as the number of languages we speak. Nevertheless, it is necessary to analyze the phenomenon of translation with more discipline. In order to do that, I shall borrow the existential term "borderline situation." K. Jaspers says that it is in this situation that Being is revealed, and he cites as an example the situation of love, sickness, defeat, or more radically, the situation of death. In these situations, I am being exposed to nothingness. The ground of reality is pulled out from under my feet, and it is in this way that I can, so to speak, transcend it. Therefore, I suggest to you that the situation of translation is exactly one of these situations, although without the dramaticism of the other borderline situations. As it is an ordinary situation, since we are all able to experience it daily and all the time, it allows for a careful analysis. As I translate, I routinely annihilate and recompose myself. I can, in this situation, experience my annihilation with the minimum of emotion, and this is perhaps why I'm able to overcome it intellectually, as I translate myself into the thought of the second language.

I can, as of now, distinguish between inauthentic and genuine translations or, as it is customary to say, between literal and meaningful translations. I give you the following example: If I translate the Portuguese phrase "*Tenho fome*" to "Have hunger," it would be an inauthentic translation, but if I translate it to "I am hungry," then it would be genuine. Thus, in the first case, I would not be in a borderline situation, because the Portuguese words would simply have been substituted by lexically correspondent words, but my phrase would continue being

Portuguese in its meaning. I would not have gone through the series of vertical translations, and I would always be a Self of the Portuguese conversation. It is therefore perfectly possible to speak Portuguese with English words. But in the second case, I would be a polyglot. I would have changed reality. It is obvious that the real situation, which the phrase "I am hungry" establishes, is different from that established by the phrase "*Tenho fome*," even though they are two adequated realities. In the English reality, hunger relates to me in a different way through the verb "to be" and not through the verb "to have," as in the Portuguese reality. These realities are, however, adequated to each other through my polyglotism. My polyglotism is the adequation of both realities. Through my polyglotism I have overcome both realities and encompassed them within me, without having created a third reality. I am me because I adequate realities. To be me, means to be the adequation between two realities, and this adequation is possible due to the vacuity of the Self. The Self has no fundament, it is "*Bodenlos*," and, in this opening toward nothingness, realities become adequated. All those among you, who have already experienced the effort of translation, will intuit what I have in mind, which is, the deliberate effort to annihilate oneself. It is necessary to eliminate my Portuguese Self, if I want to acquire the English Self, and thus, translate authentically. My will to translate is, therefore, that adequation between the two languages. And, at this point in the argument, I have to mention Schopenhauer's philosophy. For Schopenhauer, the fundament of reality is the Will. This Will is a tendency, a virtuality, and it tends toward representation through the *principium individuationis*. If we attempt to frame Schopenhauer's thought in our argument, every language would present itself to us as a different form of representation of the Will; every language would be an articulation of the unarticulated Will through the *principium individuationis*. The worlds established by languages would be realizations of this differentiated articulation. By translating, I would overcome my individuality and would dive into the unarticulated Will, only to emerge again in language, and therefore, in a different reality. I would experience, at the moment of translation, Schopenhauer's terrible concept: "*Der Wille ist Grundlos*": the Will as something that lacks motive and fundament. Schopenhauer identifies this unarticulated Will with the *Brahman* of Indian speculation, or, in other words, that pit in which I can free myself from the suffering that reality is. However, our analysis of translation overcomes, I believe, Schopenhauer's pessimism, and its implicit anti-intellectualism. You probably know that Schopenhauer affirms that we have only one-way of experiencing unarticulated Will: through music, which is the Will. And that it is through this that we are able to free ourselves from suffering. Music would be, in this case, a kind of intellectual suicide. I shall deal with this problem when we speak about poetry. However, I believe to have shown that we can experience the Will in translation, and that we can experience it intellectually. Translation is not an intellectual suicide, but it is a transfiguration of the death of the Self, through which, I have emerged enriched.

What Schopenhauer calls the Will is what Freud would later call *Libido*, Jung *The Shadow*, and Existentialism

69

Nullifying Nothingness. As we translate, we open ourselves to this nothingness, so that we may emerge from it enriched. Through translation we experience the borders of the Self. These borders are the language in which we are immersed. And, in translation, we are able to overcome these borders, although only in order to integrate ourselves again within other borders, the ones of a second language. The possibility of polyglotism multiplies the field of our realizations, without, however, elevating us above every language.

Let us now consider another aspect of the Self that has become evident. I am while I converse. I am, therefore, always in function of others. I am, because phrases from others precipitate upon me, and because my phrases precipitate upon others. This conversation that I am may be internal. In this case, it would almost be as though all the others were present. I would virtually be a multitude of personalities. But there is no contradiction in this apparent paradox. I am not a something, but a how. I am how phrases occur. The Self, when it finds itself, finds itself within a situation that always includes others. When J. Ortega y Gasset says: I am myself and my circumstance, he means, simply, to say that I am myself and others. Effectively, I am a centralizing aspect of others. It is almost as if others exist in function of me, and that I exist in function of others. I believe that it is in this aspect of the Self that the key to the problem of immortality resides. Others immortalize themselves in me, and I immortalize myself in others. Aristotle is immortal because his phrases continue to occur from a form called *I*. And he will continue being immortal because his phrases will pass from me to others. Conversation, as the sum of Selves, is immortality itself. Faith in the immortality of the soul is faith in the real fundament of the Self: the "soul." Lack of faith in immortality, or faith in definitive death, is the consequence of a false analysis of the Self. The analysis of translation has shown that I am able to overcome the nothingness that invades me. As I am a form of conversation, I am immortal, when I am among others. And at this point in the argument, it is fitting to speak of the notion of love, so characteristic of Christianity. Love for thy neighbor is a kind of love for God. I may call love that connection which unites me with the other. The love for the other is a form of love for conversation, which is the fundament of reality. And it is through this type of love that I immortalize myself intellectually. This is Spinoza's intellectual love, formalized. All of the other forms of love, and of immortality, are metaphysical, and should be eliminated from methodical discourse, although with sorrow, and perhaps with a slightly heavy conscience.

The existential analysis of translation that I sought to sketch with a few words, points toward vast horizons, because it relates to a borderline situation. I do not pretend that my analysis is exhaustive. On the contrary, I confess that we are moving through uncharted territory. But I believe to have made my initial affirmative a little more comprehensive to you; that both the external world and the Self are nothing but horizons of language. Certainly, your objections will be just as violent as your earlier objections against the elimination of the external world from a disciplined discussion. Our faith in the external world seeks arguments within the terrain of the natural sciences;

our faith in the Self seeks them within the terrain of psychology. I ask you to consider, when you formulate your arguments, that psychology is perhaps nothing more than the obverse of physics, therefore, on the other side of language. The stone outside and the impression of the stone in here, are perhaps nothing more than a way of wanting to determine the meaning of the word "stone." And it is, perhaps, from this will to want to determine the meaning of words that the external world and the Self emerge.

My argument is not valid to fight against faith, be it faith in the reality of the external world, or be it faith in the reality of the soul. My argument is a consequence of a loss of faith in both. Those of you, who by chance nurture one or both faiths, must put them in phenomenological parentheses in order to be able to follow my argument. Only then, will a conversation between us become possible.

Bibliography:
Klages, L: *Die Sprache als Quell der Seelenkunde*
Whitehead, A. N: *Modes of Thought*
Jaspers, K: *Verkunft und Existenz*
Buber, M: *Dialogisches Leben*
Jung, C. G: *Der Symbolik des Geistes*

VI. Language as an Opus

Today I shall make use of the discussion on the concept of "Self," to which we dedicated our last meeting, and I shall submit to you some considerations related to this problem. This means I shall be infringing upon the course's program, since I had scheduled an analysis of the phrase to present to you. I leave this analysis for our next meeting, so we don't lose the thread of the argument.

I shall seek to define conversation as a fabric of phrases that crisscross upon Selves. And I shall seek to identify the term "conversation" with the term "intellect." The intellect will, therefore, be the field in which phrases that link Selves occur. My purpose today, will be to widen this view of the intellect a little. In order to do so, I shall introduce two of Heidegger's terms: "*Befindlichkeit*" and "*Stimmung.*" Both terms are untranslatable. The first term relates to the moment at which I find myself, and the situation, in which I am, at that moment. The second term relates to the climate in which this encounter takes place. Given my definition of intellect, I can say that, as I find myself, I find myself in conversation, that is: my "*Befindlichkeit*" is the conversation, and it is in conversing that I exist. It must be obvious to you that this formulation is nothing but an existentialization of the Cartesian "*cogito.*"

And, given my definition of intellect, I can still say that the climate that envelops my "*Befindlichkeit*" is one of being in accord and in tune with others: "*übereinstimmen mit anderen.*" As I find myself, I find myself in vibration (*Stimmung*) with others, and this vibration, this sympathy, evokes in me the sensation of certainty in a particular reality, the sensation of "*das stimmt*" (that is correct). My "*Befindlichkeit*" in conversation is the fundament of my "*Stimmung*" as existence in a situation of reality. Conversation is a field in which I find myself with others, in a climate of reality. Conversation is the fundament of my being here in reality. I am, really me, because I concord with others, conversing. The fundament of my reality is an accord with others. It is in virtue of this accord, of this covenant, of this conversation, of this "*Stimmung,*" that I find myself here, that I "*befinde*" myself. It is in this sense that I am able to say that language is a product of a covenant: that it is conventional: that it is the product of an accord in relation to its meaning. Language, which is the sum of all conversations, is the articulation of a covenant, due to which I find myself. This accord that establishes language, and continues to establish languages forever, is veiled to me if I find myself at the center of the conversation, surrounded by others on all sides. But if I find myself at the border of the conversation, at its margin, in a borderline situation, then this fundamental accord, this "*Stimmung*" of language, starts to become unveiled. If I find myself in a borderline situation, if my "*Befindlichkeit*" is a borderline one, I shall vibrate with the "*Stimmung*" of the origin of language. Last Friday I sought to clarify one of these borderline situations, the one in which I find myself when I translate from one language to another. To-day, I shall clarify a different situation.

There is an essay by Heidegger, called *Wozu Dichter?* (Wherefore poets?), which illustrates, appealing to Hölderlin, the situation I have in mind. Given the deficiency of my being here, given my vacuity and openness toward the nothingness that surrounds conversation, it could be, I must say, that I may not be perfectly in tune with others. I am not in accord with others; I am not in agreement with them. I do not really find myself, I am not really here, and none of this is reality. This is the climate of the "*da stimmt etwas nicht*" (something is not correct). In this climate, in which I desperately try to find myself, in which I cannot find myself with others, I project myself out of the conversation, toward its border. In this project, I become an "outsider," I remain at the margin of that, which for others is reality. I alienate myself; I court madness. It could be that I never find myself in this project. In this case, I shall fall from conversation into a word salad and the mumbling of madness. This is the danger of my project, which emerges from the climate of "something is not correct." That is why Guimarães Rosa says, "To live, is very dangerous." But it could be that, in my project, I suddenly find myself. Now imagine that I find myself, in this sudden finding, at the edge of the abyss, one step away from madness; that I find myself, finding myself, facing nothingness; that my "*Befindlichkeit*" is the limit of language. In this situation, a climate, a vibration, that is not a vibrating with others, but a vibrating with nothingness, emerges. I am in accord and in accordance with nothingness; I am in tune with nothingness. This is the unarticulated, the totally different from me, the totally Other, with which I am vibrating. Dilthey calls this vibration, this climate, this "*Stimmung*": "*Urschauder*" (fear of the origin). This is the climate of poetry. This point, which separates the conversation from the unarticulated, the intellect from madness, the cosmos from chaos, is a situation, the "*Befindlichkeit*" of poetry. And it is at this point that conversation emerges, that the intellect emerges, that reality emerges and that the accord with the totally different, which fundaments language, establishes itself. Poets are the intellect's advanced post, they establish the accord with the totally different in order to transform it into language. And it is in this sense that the ancients would say poets are the mouthpieces of the muses, and that it is through the prophets that God speaks. And it is also at this point, in virtue of the poets, that the adequation between the intellect and the totally different happens, which is called, "truth."

Please forgive me if I have allowed myself to be instantly carried away by enthusiasm. I promise that I shall know how to withhold, in the following argument, the enthusiasm that the contemplation of poetry provokes in me. Before seeking to analyze what happens at the moment of poetry, please allow me to appeal to humanity's great myths. The moment I am describing is that which alludes to the myth of Prometheus, who takes the fire from the alter of the gods; the moment of Moses' wandering in the desert, where he finds himself fighting flames; the platonic wise man, who returns to the cave of conversation, obfuscated by the sun of knowledge; Zarathustra who climbs his mountain, having abandoned the plain of conversation; and (why not?), Nietzsche himself. These myths prefigure poetry's project. Poetry is a movement that has three phases. In the first one, poetry abandons conversation, in a search for the encounter with oneself. This first phase has, at its base, the climate of "something is not correct." In the second, poetry encounters oneself at the edge of the abyss. This second phase has, at its base, the climate of fear and trembling of the origin. And in the final phase, it returns to conversation, with the stamp of the totally different impressed upon the Self, in the form of verse. This third phase has, at its base, the climate of truth, of "*das stimmt*" (it is correct). The triple nature of its movement distinguishes poetry from prayer. Prayer also projects itself from conversation, but never to return. That is why we, who find ourselves in conversation, feel the productivity of poetry, but experience prayer as a loss. However, it is obvious, given the structure of both processes, that poetry and prayer are similar linguistic phenomena. We could, perhaps, frame Saint Thomas' silence within this context, and perhaps the Wittgensteinian silence also.

I shall seek to approach the problem of poetry from the problem of truth. Traditional philosophy defines truth as the adequation of the intellect to the thing. However, it is obvious that this definition is an entreaty from the start, because it presupposes that this adequation happens in the intellect itself. The intellect is, for traditional philosophy, the collection of thoughts. The thing, to which the intellect must adequate itself, is not thought. However, the adequation itself is thought. But, if the adequation is thought (or a quality of thought), it is then a case of one or the other: (1) either we do not have criteria to distinguish between adequated thoughts and non-adequated ones, or (2) these criteria are beyond the intellect. We are, therefore, facing the problem of the criterion of adequation; therefore, at the starting point. We must, idiotically repeat, that the criterion for the adequation of the intellect to the thing, is, the adequation of the intellect to the thing. We have two possible exits from this situation: we could say that the criterion for the adequation is an intuitive faculty of which we dispose, and that we could locate this faculty either in the senses, or internally. Or we could say that adequated thoughts are the ones that result in adequate behavior. Notice what has happened. We are no longer saying that truth is the adequation of the intellect to the thing but that it is, in the first case, the adequation of the intellect to the senses and, in the second case, of the intellect to behavior. However, both empiricism and pragmatism continue as prisoners of that primitive difficulty. If neither the senses nor behavior is an integral part of the intellect, then what is the intellectual criterion in order to distinguish between adequated thoughts and non-adequated ones? Therefore, the substitution of the thing by the senses or behavior has not helped, even though it has brought valuable contributions to the comprehension of the process of knowledge.

However, if I substitute the terms "senses" and "behavior" with "poetry," I shall have created a new type of empiricism and pragmatism, because poetry is an integral part of the intellect. I shall have, henceforth, an intellectual criterion to distinguish between adequated thoughts and non-adequated ones. I shall say that adequated thoughts are verses. I shall be able to say that the intellect adequates itself to what is totally different from itself (which I shall not call "thing" because I cannot name the totally different, due to its total difference); I shall be able, therefore, to say that the intellect adequates itself to the totally different, which, for being totally different, is the nothingness that adequates itself through poetry. And I shall be able to say something in reference to this adequation: that it happens in the climate of trembling of the origin, and that it is original in this sense. This is not, therefore, an adequation of the intellect to some given set (for example: a set of things), but an adequation of the intellect to the amorphous nothingness of virtualities, from which, upon the very act of adequation, the intellect wrenches pieces of reality. The intellect produces reality as it adequates itself to the totally different. Truth is an aspect of the production of reality, and not a passive acceptance of a given reality. By knowing, I produce, and by producing, I know. This is poetry. It is within this context that we should frame Nietzsche's famous phrase "*Kunst ist besser als Wahrheit*" (Art is better than truth).

As an example of what I am trying to say, let us take the experience of our Vietnamese friend, which we sought to discuss last Friday, without permission. He looks through a telescope and sees the moon. At least he does that, which I have just said, in Portuguese, within a Portuguese reality. This Portuguese reality is the consequence of a reality of a conversation that emerged and continues to emerge from a series of myths, and myths are ancient verses. Poetry productively wrenched, thousands of years ago, pieces of the totally different, of nothingness, and threw these pieces into the conversation that we are. In the course of this conversation, these verses were elaborated, conversed, elucidated, and the telescope and the moon are products of this process. Fundamentally, things such as the telescope and the moon were produced by the productive activity of poetry.

The telescope and the moon are prefigured in the myths of our antiquity. For example: both the telescope and the moon are material things, because matter is a consequence of the elaboration of our verses. The telescope is an artificial thing, an instrument, and the moon is a natural thing, because art and nature were elaborated by the conversation that we are. We exist in nature and technology, because poetry established our reality in this way. And all of this is true because, as it established this world, poetry vibrated with the all-different. Our Vietnamese friend does what I have just said, that is, he looks at the moon through a telescope because, he too, is part of that reality which our poetry established.

Let us now attempt the extremely difficult task of describing the same occurrence from the Vietnamese point of view. Our friend is located, he finds himself, in an entirely different reality, because it was established by different myths, by different verses, by a poetry that vibrates differently with nothingness. In this reality there is no matter, no nature, no art; therefore, there is also no telescope and no moon in this reality. There are probably not even things, in this reality, only situations that are in some way relatable to our situations. Why is the Vietnamese situation relatable to ours? That is because it emerged from the same amorphous pit as ours; because it is also truthful, since the poetry that established the Vietnamese reality vibrates with the same fundament, although in a different form. It is another reality, with other truths, but the inarticulable fundament is the same. This common, inarticulable fundament, allows me to say that the Vietnamese person looks, through the telescope, at the moon. Perhaps he will say that the spirits of his ancestors brought the nocturnal water shepherd close to him, because certain gestures forced them to do so. And that this nocturnal shepherd has been hurt by bombings, identical to those that castigate whoever does not please the spirits in the appropriate manner, as the current invasion, by the suppliers of voracious fish called "Americans" demonstrates. It is obvious that I do not insist that this is exactly the Vietnamese experience, and that I sought only to sketch a caricature of a reality that could be different from ours. And that the judgments formulated within it will obey a different criterion of truth, because the vibration of poetry was different. Thus, I believe, the different languages emerged, with their different realities. And this is why I believe that translations between different languages, with different structures, are practically impossible: one cannot translate between two different truths. These worlds are different because they are the result of different types of poetry.

You will have noticed that the exposition I have just offered you is nothing but a reformulation of the theses exposed when the proper name was our theme. Effectively, I had already sought, in that context, to give a formal definition of the verse as a phrase that predicates new proper names. But in the current context, you will be able to grasp what I mean, when I say, "new proper name." The new proper name is the articulation of the intellect's vibration with the nothingness that surrounds it. The new proper name is the stamp of the unarticulated upon the intellect. And if we appeal to a myth: the new proper name is the Ten Commandments, with which Moses returns from the mountain. Poetry is that place, at the borders of conversation, where new proper names emerge. But the verse is not only a new proper name. It is the elevation of this name to the subject of a predicative phrase, at least according to our project of languages. Poetry frames, within our project, the proper name in a "*sui generis*" structure called, "verse," and this structure will be the structure of our reality. Thanks to the verse's structure (which will be the theme of my next exposition), our reality and our intellect have a logical character, as well as one of analytic geometry, which in the course of the conversation, will enable the emergence of the sciences as methods for analyses and manipulations of reality.

In this exposition, I sought to come closer to the problem of poetry from two different sides, that is: from immediate experience and from the theoretical attempt to define the term "truth." Through the first prism, poetry emerged as the encounter of the Self with itself, (*Befindlichkeit*) at the intellect's border, and as the climate (*Stimmung*) of trembling from the origin. Through the prism of truth, poetry emerged as that movement of the intellect through which the intellect productively adequates itself to that which is entirely different. However, we could assume a third point of view, a historical point of view, and focus on poetry as the historical origin of language. We could say, by framing the problem in this way, that language emerged "*in illo tempore*" as an articulation, an expression, an expulsion from the unarticulated fundament. This expulsion (of which, perhaps, the myth of paradise speaks to us) would be like the first encounter with oneself. The unarticulated and virtual, unformed fundament, would thus expel the creative word from its bosom, in order to find itself and become established as reality. This would be the accord and the covenant that established language: to realize the virtuality, dormant in nothingness. Language, intellect, thought — or in other words, man as a thinking being — would have emerged as the poetic articulation of Being, so that Being could establish itself as Being, and not as nothingness.. The irruption of language would be a poetic and creative unveiling of Being, and it would be, in this sense, that we could say that man, as a participant of conversation, is the point at which Being becomes realized. The origin of language (which is the origin of human thought), would be, in Heidegger's words, that emergence of the clear night of the anguish of nothingness, in which things show themselves for what they are, that is, things, and not, nothingness. This first poetic articulation would be the outing of Being, up until now veiled, and with this outing a new proper history would begin, that is, history as a process of projected realizations.

Effectively, the history of our civilization seems to prove this vision of poetry. It emerges from the myth's penumbra, from the dense and impenetrable verse, and the climate that surrounded this origin of civilization is the climate of trembling that characterizes poetry. As it advances, as it converses the myths that projected it, our civilization elucidates, loosens, and prosifies primordial verses, realizing their projects. In the process, those progressively prosaic stages that we generally call religious, philosophical, scientific, and technological, emerge. The climate of original trembling dilutes and the climate of doubt, of untuning, of "*da stimmt etwas nicht,*" becomes established. The progressive realization of the primordial project is a continuous alienation of thought from its origins. This is why the greater the progress, the greater the climate of absurdity, since "absurd" means "far from the roots." But the progressive conversation, which our civilization is, is not fated to the total realization of the projects contained in its myths; our civilization is not fated to the realization of that Earthly Paradise that technology and communism promise, and which will be total prosification: an unbearable tedium, with the sensation of absurdity that accompanies paradise. Our civilization is not fated to this, because we, the Selves in conversation, are defective beings, open toward nothingness, open toward poetry. We exist, that is, we always transcend our situation through our vacuity. And because of this vacuity we always intuit that something is out of tune. We are all, as authentic existences, potential poets, and we may, always project ourselves toward borderline situations. Of course we may always fallback, we may always close ourselves, become full of ourselves, satisfied with the situation, and, in this climate of inauthenticity, precipitate ourselves toward death. In this situation, we would be deaf to poetry. But given our vacuity, we may always decide in favor of poetry. And in poetry, we may always reestablish contact with our origin, with truth, and with the all-different that surrounds our situation and invades our inner core at every instant. In other words, finding ourselves depends upon our own decision to do so. Poetry is the source from which our civilization always renews itself. The verses that poetry verts upon conversation, in a vivifying rain, are the places where we shall always encounter ourselves.

As I said, the first step of this decision in favor of poetry is a projection of the Self out of conversation; a decision in favor of alienation, of self-absorption [*ensimesmamento*]; a search for solitude, because the all-different becomes manifest only in solitude. Don Miguel de Unamuno y Jugo articulates this decision in favor of poetry in a wonderful way:

> *Soledad de soledades,*
> > *soledad!*
> *¡Me he perdido de mí mismo*
> > *la verdad!*
>
> *¿Es que he muerto sin saberlo,*
> > *soledad?*
> *¿Es que vivía viviendo*
> > *mi soñar?*
>
> *¿Mi voz me llega de fuera,*
> > *quién la da?*
> *¿quién es el que así me llama?*
> > *Dios sabrá...*[6]

Loneliness of all lonelinesses, /loneliness! / The truth has been lost from my self! / Am I unknowingly dead, / loneliness? / Had I been living my own dreaming? / My voice, it comes to me from without,

I believe that the theory of poetry I have sought to expose to you is contained, as a whole, in these verses. And I re-define, therefore, the Self: the Self is that knot of phrases in the conversation, which is open toward nothingness, and through this opening, poetry can irrupt in order to enrich the conversation and propel it toward new realizations. And it is through the same vacuity that language irrupted, "*in illo tempore*," as the first encounter of Being with itself. I hope that this excurse toward existentialist thought has given you more possibilities to locate the type of philosophy that I am attempting to expose.

Bibliography:
Heidegger, M. *Was ist das, die Philosophie?*
Kierkegaard, S. *Fear and Trembling*
Sartre, JP. *Being and Nothingness*
Jaspers, K. *Ein philosophische Glaube*

/ who speaks? / Who is it that calls me thus? / God knows... (My translation.) [TN]

VII. Conversation

Allow me to recapitulate, in a few words, the situation of the argument with which we are engaged. Our starting point was the theory of knowledge with the classic problem of the relation between knower and known. In the attempt to overcome this difficulty, we took Kant as a base, because all of the other philosophical positions seem to imply, if radicalized, one or another type of skepticism. The discussion of the Kantian position led us to identify the categories of reality and of knowledge as the rules of language. This identification suggested a theory of knowledge, according to which, knowledge would be anterior to knower and known. In other words: knower and known would be two aspects of the process of knowledge. Other considerations led us to identify this knowledge with the discourse of language. Afterwards, we extrapolated the problem to the field of ontology, in which known became "the external world" and knower "I." Our argument sought, therefore, the plausibility of the idea that the external world and I are two aspects of discourse, and ontologically posterior to it. In the course of our argument, several difficulties emerged, which largely related to the multiplicity of existent languages. Given the ontological position that language occupied in our argument, this multiplicity of languages was equivalent to a fragmentation of fundamental reality, which shocked our Parmenidean prejudices. In the attempt to save at least the appearance of unity, we discussed the problem of translation from both a formal and existential point of view. We verified, therefore, in this discussion, the limitations of language as being a reality surrounded by nothingness. This discussion led us to consider the borderline situations of language, which we identified, through an existential analysis, with the situations of poetry. We are, thus, at the following point in our argument: fundamental reality is a language that becomes established from nothingness through poetic creation (which is an articulation of this nothingness), and this language has two aspects called "external world" and "I." Given the multiplicity of languages, we are forced to concede that there are as many external worlds as there are languages, however, the possibility of translation seems to guarantee a certain problematic connection between this diversity of realities. Let us proceed with the argument.

If we have given credit to the argument, up until now, we are obliged to identify linguistic analysis with ontological analysis, although the term "linguistic analysis" should have, obviously, a wider scope than the one it has within the context of logic. I shall dedicate the discussion today to the consideration of this type of analysis, and I shall restrict the discussion to the Portuguese language. I have already said that this language offers its analyzer two levels of analysis, that is, the level of the word and that of the phrase. It is, in the end, this characteristic that we mean when we call this language "fusional." At the level of the word we can generally distinguish three types of words: substantives and their derivates, verbs and their derivates, and logical words. At the level of the phrase we can generally distinguish three structures: subject, predicate, and object. As I have already briefly discussed the type of words called "substantives," and especially proper names, I intend to start this analysis with the consideration of the type of words I have called "verbs."

I have already said that the verb is the nucleus of the predicate, and that, as our language is predicative; it is in the verb that we shall discover the structure of the situation established by the phrase. I shall define "verb" as the type of word that indicates the manner in which the substantive, elevated as the subject of the phrase, finds itself (*sich befindet*). The verb can be inflected through "conjugation," and in this inflection, two forms emerge: finite and infinite. In the finite form we can distinguish (1) person, (2) number, (3) tense, (4) mode, and (5) gender. I shall not consider the infinitive form, because it is nothing but a variant of substantives, for example the infinitive, participle, and gerundive. However, the problem of the substantiation of verbs is complex, and may be discussed on another occasion.

In Portuguese there are, effectively, only two persons: the *I* and the *Other*. The *I* is asexual, and the *Other* has two genders. Vestiges of the *tu* [you *sing.*] and *vós* [you *pl.*], and the tendencies to eliminate these vestiges from the discourse, characterize our language.

In Portuguese there are two kinds of grammatical numbers: the singular and the plural. The dual and trial have been eliminated, and the Slavic quadral has never existed.

The Portuguese tense, which is hugely complex and contrasts with the simplicity of persons and numbers, has, among others, the following forms: present, past (perfect, imperfect, and pluperfect), future, future perfect, conditional, and vestiges of the aorist.

The Portuguese modes are, approximately, the indicative, subjunctive (conjunctive), and imperative. As incredible as it may seem for someone from the Germanic or Slavic languages, the mode of becoming does not exist.

Portuguese genders are impoverished down to two: active (m) and passive (f). And the passive tends to be superseded.

If we cast a glance at this apparently exhaustive list, which is of fundamental importance for the analysis of our reality, we can verify that the main tendency of the Portuguese language is to reduce all of the characteristics of *Befindlichkeit* from Being down to two: time and mode. I do not believe that it is possible to exaggerate the importance of this discovery at first glance.

A few extra considerations about the verb: In Portuguese there are some auxiliary verbs, for example the verbs *ter, ir, haver, estar, ficar,* and *ser,*[7] which endow the

---

7. *Ter, ir, ficar* and *ser* are easily translated as *to have, to go, to stay,* and *to be.* But *haver* and *estar* are verbs that point to particular modes of Being within the verb to be, which are often translated as different forms of *there being.* However, this differentiation is not clearly defined since the differences are very subtle and can be employed in several different forms depending on the context. For example, *haver* points toward the presence of something in a kind of existential sense, but it can also mean to have in some contexts. And *estar* also points toward the presence of something, although in more of a material sense, but it can also have an existential dimension. Additionally, *estar* is

Portuguese reality with a characteristic structure. It is still possible to distinguish further aspects of the verb, of which I shall mention only the intransitive verbs, which do not demand an object, and the transitive verbs, which do demand an object. (The subject could become such an object, when we speak of reflexive verbs.) It is obvious that these aspects of the verb establish different situations of reality.

As for the logical words, I shall say only, so as not to turn this exposition too boring, that their symbolization through symbolic logic represses the entire existential aura that surrounds them and that characterize the Portuguese language. Consider for example, some of the forms of "if then," symbolized by the arrow: "*por causa de,*" "*em virtude de,*" "*graças a,*" "*devido a,*" etc. [because of, in virtue of, thanks to, due to]. And as for the substantives, I only remember that it is possible to reduce them down to two types: "proper names" and "common names" whose medieval problematic we have already discussed.

If my argument has any validity, then this sketched classification of words and their aspects should form the starting point for any analysis of Being worthy of its name. But do not fear; I do not intend to start it here. This would be a task that surpasses the scope of a lifetime. Effectively, it seems to me that this is the task of a philosophy of Being that has yet to come. Words and their forms are the very foundational stones from which situations of reality will become constituted in the form of phrases. I can,

---

close to Heidegger's *Dasein*, in that it fuses the temporal and material dimensions of Being into one. Hence the difficulty of rendering these two verbs in English. [TN]

therefore, now return to a discussion of the phrase, started in our third meeting, but suspended for lack of elements.

You may remember that I discussed the form of the phrase in the example "*João ama Maria.*" At the time I said that this phrase establishes a situation of reality, and I therefore called "reality" precisely the situation that the phrase establishes. I said, furthermore, that this situation has the form of a project, because the predicate projects itself from subject to object, within it. I called this project "predicative." I can now add that this project of realization concretizes virtualities dormant in the words that compose the phrase, and that it realizes only some of those virtualities. And I say, also, that it can only realize those virtualities that the words shelter, and not others. In other words: the phrase is a predicative project that realizes virtualities sheltered by words of the Portuguese language. The collection of phrases as a whole is called "the Portuguese language's discourse," and the collection of its realizations is called the "external world," as established by the Portuguese language's discourse.

Today my aim is to discuss with you the dynamic that propels predicative projects, or, phrases. In order to do that, first, it is necessary to consider the term "project." I am seeking, by using this term, to translate the German word "*Entwurf*" to Portuguese, which is one of the fundamental concepts of Existentialism. I discussed this term briefly, together with poetry. For existentialist thought, every realization is a turning against the fundament of my Being, which threw me here toward death. This turning against one's own origin is an "*Entwurf*," a kind of "defecating of oneself." It is in this sense that I employ the term "project." When I turn myself against my origin, I separate myself from it, I distance myself from it, I create an abyss between myself and my origin, in order to throw myself against it afterwards. Effectively, when I turn, I transform my origin into my object, and myself into subject, and the throwing of myself into a predicate. When I turn against my origin, I am engaged in a project, which is simply the standard phrase of my language. My decision not to fall back toward death, to oppose myself to my unarticulated fundament, and to impose myself upon it, is, in the end, my decision to engage myself in my language's discourse. To speak existentially: my decision to be myself, to find myself, and to realize myself as an authentic existence, is, in the end, my decision in favor of conversation, in favor of thought. It is only within conversation that I realize myself and it is, therefore, only within thought and with thought that I project myself. As you can see, our analysis of the phrase, when applied to the existential context, results in the exact opposite conclusion than those the existentialists arrived at. An analysis of the phrase, which is an analysis of thought, existentially validates thought as the only authentic project, and results in creative intellectualism, instead of resulting in the existentialists' anti-intellectualism.

The dynamic that propels the predicative project, or phrase, is therefore, the dynamic of my decision not to fall and to say no to death. Discourse as a whole, this entire majestic chain of phrases, is, in the end, a single gigantic "no" to death. Discourse is, in this sense, a chain of negative projects. I read in A.J. Ayer and in Vicente Ferreira da Silva that every logical form can be reduced to a form of "no" and that it is, therefore, possible to prove formally that discourse is a negative project. Prof. Hegenberg may confirm or refute this affirmative. However, it is not necessary to formally prove what we experience, if we are attentive to what happens when we think: that is, we think against death. In the end, death is our exclusive subject, and everything we say is said in order to negate death. I can, therefore, define the phrase as a predicative project against death.

If we accept this definition, we will have a base for an existential analysis of discourse. I said that the phrase is a predicative project. I have already discussed the concept of predicating in a formal context, in which I defined predication as the progressive explication of proper names toward common names. In the present context I can add that predication is a negation of the proper name, because it progressively empties its meaning. Discourse is a chain of predicative projects against death, because as it predicates proper names into verbs, it also empties these proper names of meaning and establishes them in situations of reality according to the virtualities contained in the verbs. Death presents itself to us, in this context, as what is behind the proper name, or, as that nothingness from which the proper name has been taken by poetry. Discourse is a critique of verses, proposed by poetry, but in an opposite direction, in the sense of distancing thought from the borderline situation of the proper name. And this situation is, in the last analysis, a confrontation with death. By progressively predicating, the discourse distances itself from the borderline situation of death, and in this progressive distancing it creates reality. Reality is the protective cover that the discourse establishes around itself in the course of its progress, to cover ("*vorstellen*") its negative subject: death. In this sense, as a distancing from the borderline situation, discourse is a critique of the verses of poetry: it prosifies. I can, therefore, complete my definition of phrase in the following manner: the phrase is a predicative project against death through progressive prosification. The measure of prosification is the establishment of situations of reality.

If we attempt to summarize this predicative project against death through progressive prosification in a single term, this term will be "doubt." Our formal and existential analysis of the phrase is, in the end, an analysis of *doubt*. Doubt is the "*Befindlichkeit*" in which we find ourselves due to our decision to negate death. And doubt has the structure and the climate of the phrase. Our existential project, through which we realize ourselves, and through which we establish situations of reality, is our doubting of what threw us here, and it has the form and climate of the phrase. Effectively, when Descartes says we are things that think, he is affirming that our project is the predication of proper names into verbs toward common names, and that we are, therefore, things that doubt. Our doubt is a creative project, as long as it prosifies, that is, as long as it establishes situations of reality. However, it is a closed project, because it can only realize virtualities contained in the verb. The renewal of this project, the emergence of new virtualities for realization, is not possible through discourse. We cannot, if engaged in discourse, open up new realization projects. This renewal comes to us through the verses of poetry, which continuously throws new proper names upon the discourse, which continuously predicates them into new verbs. In other words: poetry always provides new subjects to be discussed, that is, doubted and transformed into situations of reality. Discourse is a progressive and prosifying conversion of verses into situations of reality. In the last analysis, however, every subject that poetry puts here to be doubted is an articulation of the negation of death.

So as not to leave the subject which I am developing hovering above the terrain of theory, I propose a quick consideration of that discourse upon which we are engaged as participants of that conversation called "Western civilization." However, I shall consider only its last phase that begins with the Renaissance. The "*Befindlichkeit*" of the Renaissance, or how man found himself at that stage of our conversation, was characterized by the opening of new projects.

The subjects contained in the verses of the Bible and in Aristotle had been highly prosified and no longer gave margin for predicative realizations. The conversation of these projects began to become repetitive, that is, to become small talk. At that moment, new verses to be doubted emerged; therefore, a new opening for progressive predication emerged. The subject of the new verses was the circumstance in which man found himself. This circumstance had not been the subject of Medieval verses, and in this sense, it was a new subject. The Renaissance directed its doubt against its circumstance, and no longer against itself, or against the "soul," which had been the subject of previous verses. Doubt, directed against this circumstance, transformed it into a subject, that is, into something objective called "nature." Thus, that discourse called "the natural sciences" emerged from such methodically predicative doubt. The "*Befindlichkeit*" of the Renaissance was precisely this creative doubt that had nature as a subject. Therefore, the proper names from the verses that put nature here were objects, and the verbs that predicated these proper names toward classes were how these objects could come to be. This structure of Renaissance phrases established situations of reality that could be called "Mechanistic." The first prosification of Renaissance verses resulted in a collection of situations of reality, in which the circumstance had been realized as a mechanism. Once this situation had been established, Western conversation found itself in a "*Befindlichkeit*" called "Baroque." The subject of the Baroque was already prosified; it was nature as a mechanism. The progressive predication of this subject tended to simplify this mechanism and resulted in the realization of a set of situations of reality that we could call "simple apparatus." In this set of situations, conversation found itself in that "*Befindlichkeit*" called "Enlightenment." At that moment, conversation found itself in danger of exhausting its subject and of falling into that small talk called "preciousness." At this stage of conversation a new verb was introduced, which gave the old subject a new structure. It was the verb "to become" or "*werden*." Discourse started to reformulate all of its phrases with this verb, starting at its mathematical level, and later at every level, and, from this reformulation, a new set of situations of reality emerged, which we could call "organism." Within this set, conversation found itself in a new "*Befindlichkeit*" called "Romanticism." From this stage of conversation all verbs, except this one, were progressively eliminated, and with this verb, proper names were predicated as increasingly more general common names. It is obvious that the discourse's progress did not develop in parallel at every level, however, at some levels, the prosification and realization reached a stage in which doubt no longer has a subject. Today we find ourselves in a set of situations of reality without a subject, that is, without meaning, and this climate could be called "absurd." The verb "to become" (or, as we say, the process oriented way of establishing situations of reality), predicates names of a high level of generality, which endows our situation with an abstract and theoretical quality, and tends to transform our phrases into tautologies, especially in the field of mechanics and other rigorous sciences. The exhaustion of the subject, doubt's impossibility to fix itself upon a subject, makes death reappear as a borderline situation, and because we cannot doubt, we fall toward it. We need new poets.

It is obvious that the manner in which I described what, in the last analysis, is a history of the Modern Age, is nothing but a summarization and an extremely simplified sketch of a complex development. And my intention here was purely to illustrate a theory of my own. The formal and existential analysis of phrases, which I am advocating, cannot be applied in such a rudimentary way. In this context I draw your attention toward Dilthey's philosophy. For him, sciences that study what I have called discourse in our context, and which he calls "*Geist*," therefore *Geistwissenschaften*, should be established. This is what we call, very inappropriately here, "the humanities." For Dilthey, these sciences will have a psychological bent, which I believe to have avoided according to my exposition. The sciences of the spirit will have, if I am in any way correct in my exposition, formal and existential studies of phrases that compose the discourse. These studies will, if successful, shed light upon the genesis and structure of the realities that discourse establishes around itself, as it doubts its subjects. And, at last, the natural sciences will be nothing but the study of a given type of reality, that is, the type which Western conversation established in its discourse from the Renaissance.

However, here I should leave a word of warning. The "sciences of the spirit" is an inappropriate term, because the term science suggests a progressive discourse, that is, one that predicates proper names toward common names. The discipline I have in mind would be a reflexive discourse, because it would predicate common names toward proper names, in order to recompose their meaning instead of explicating it. This discourse would not consist of explicative phrases, like science, but of phrases that endow meaning. Effectively, it would be a reflection of language upon itself, and I intend to dedicate the following meeting to this theme.

Bibliography:
Husserl, E. *Untersuchungen zur Phänomenologie und Theorie der Eerkenntnis*
Rickert, H. *Logik des Prädikats und das Problem der Ontologie*
Vossler, K. *Geist und Kultur in der Sprache*
Cassirer, E. *Das Erkenntnisproblem in der Philosophie und Wissenshcaft der neueren Zeit*
Schrödinger, E. *Space-Time Structure*

VIII. Existence Realizes Itself Conversing

Once again, you have diverted the course I had planned for my exposition, this time by provoking a discussion on myth. You have thus transferred the argument from the terrain of theory to that of history, but alas, I believe that this transferal, forced by you, is salutary. Now we shall have the opportunity to see whether the theory I am exposing works. Please allow me to start my exposition with a brief consideration of the importance that the concept of myth has had lately within several specialized scientific fields. As you know, the 18th century considered mythical thought as an overcome stage of human thought, and therefore, did not pay it any rigorous attention. Romanticism reacted against this rejection of myth, and its effort could be interpreted as an effort to re-mythify the world. This attention that Romanticism dedicated to myth generated interest in the study of myth on several levels of meaning. The first to seek to define the term "myth" within, let us say, a historical terrain, was J.J. Bachofen in his first major work *Mutterrecht und Urreligion*, as follows: "Myth is the exegesis of symbols that articulate the primordial lived experience of a people." As historical studies widened our horizon, and as we discovered that the five or six millennia of the so-called "historical era" were

101

nothing but a short episode within a historical process that lasted hundreds of thousands of years, it became increasingly obvious that an explanation of history is impossible without taking into consideration the primordial myths that started it. In other words, and to appeal to Bachofen, it became increasingly clear, from a certain point of view, that our history was nothing but a progressive exegesis of symbols that articulate the primordial experience of peoples from which we descend. Simultaneously, other societies were discovered and studied, and it was found that these societies existed in realities entirely divergent from ours, with values entirely divergent from ours. Our belief in the universal validity of our reality and values crumbled with the contemplation of these realities and values. The enormous diversity of these realities and systems of values becomes explicable due to the diversity of myths that fundament different societies. In this context I draw your attention to the major work of Sir. J. Frazer *The Golden Bough*, and to the penetrating and more recent studies by Károly Kerényi and Mircea Eliade. The reflexive effect of these let us say, ethnological studies, was to reinforce the hypothesis that myths will enable us to comprehend our society and ourselves. This hypothesis became even more plausible with Leo Viktor Frobenius' studies of African peoples, which demonstrated that every human activity, as rational and pragmatic as it may seem, is nothing but the ritualization of certain well determined myths; that, at last, thought and action are nothing but ritual rationalizations of myths. Added to this is the revolutionary discovery by C. Jung, perhaps the most important discovery of the 20th century: the fact that we shelter in our subconscious a layer that consists of forms that are common to all members of our society, therefore, an impersonal layer called "collective unconscious," and that this layer is nothing but a set of myths that established our society. Jung calls these unconscious myths "archetypes," and I must confess that their emergence in dreams and in madness is highly frightening. For example, an almost illiterate maid in Zurich dreams of the myth of Isis in all of its details, which was discovered by Egyptologists three years after the dream. A paranoid man from Basel draws the serpent-mother; found ten years later in Chaldea. A child of three years of age makes a paper crown, whose prototype is found later in the Hittite capital. There are more examples. Anyway, what Jung discovered, was that what we individually call "conscience," and collectively "civilization," is nothing but a thin layer, precariously overlaid onto a solid structure of myths, and that this structure informs and rules our thought and behavior. It is important to note that Jung discovered in the "collective unconscious" only those myths that are historically linked to our society, and never myths from other societies. For example, the myth of the dragon, which is so important in the East as a beneficial force, is not repeated in the Western subconscious, where the reptile is always associated with anxiety and disgust. To this, it should also be added the philological and etymological studies that seek to reconstruct the languages from which ours were formed, and that make us believe that our words are the result of a few roots, all of which related to particular myths. For example, the Indo-Germanic root "*Kel*" from which the English words "holy" and "hell" descend, and the words "*solus*" and "*salus,*" which relate to the myth of the cave, as in "hole." And lastly, I want to mention the work of C. Lévi-Strauss, which I do not know, and to which, Prof. Bento Prado recently drew my attention. It seems to me that Lévi-Strauss affirms that all of humanity's myths are variants of a few, theoretically calculable, primordial phonetic data. It is therefore obvious that the concept of myth has occupied, lately, a prominent place within the studies of several disciplines.

However, it is within the body of philosophical thought that I intend to locate the problem. In his major work *The Dawn of Philosophy*, G. Misch puts forward the thesis that philosophy is nothing but one among three exegeses of fundamental myths, which he called "*Urworte*" (original words), with the other two exegeses being religion and art. For Misch, our civilization is the synthesis of three fundamental myths contained in the following verses: "*Tat tvam asi*" (you are this), "*gnothi seauton*" (know thyself), and "*ani Jehová*" (I am who I am), and our history is nothing but a progressive attempt to synthesize, by explicating, these three myths. Thus, from this perspective, all three myths could be synthesized in the term "the myth of the subject," and, therefore, its focus would be the mythical figure of the Christ, the objectified subject, or as we say, the verb turned flesh. The proper history of the West, that is, the one that starts with Christianity and with the establishment of the Roman empire, would then be nothing but a progressive ritualization of the myth of Christ, and in this sense, an "*imitatio Christi.*" And, the technological phase, which we currently cross, would be nothing but a ritual realization of this myth in nature, and our instruments and machines would be nothing but the incarnation of the verb within a particular myth called "applied science." Scientific thought would be nothing but mythical thought, within a particular ritual, already prefigured in myth. In other words: the technological achievements that we witness today would already be prefigured in some way in the myth of Christ, and projected upon us through the progressive ritualization we call "Western history."

Misch and his followers, who elaborated the view that I am offering you, are Diltheans. Their philosophy is historicist, but also strongly influenced by Phenomenology. However, their influence on existentialist thought is enormous. Allow me to expose this thought within the current context. When I find myself, I find myself within a specific situation. What does this term, "specific," mean? It means that I am thrown into a prefigured situation, which forces all of my thoughts and activities into a certain number of pre-established channels. I shall appeal to an image so as to illustrate what I am saying. As I find myself, I find myself thrown on a stage where a play is being presented. As I find myself, I find several masks at my disposal, which I am invited to wear in order to act out several roles in the play that is underway. These masks are called "persons" (from "*persona,*" which means mask in Latin theatre). I may choose, although problematically, from the masks and roles offered in the play. My freedom resides in this choice. I may, for example, choose the mask of President of the Republic, or the mask of garbage collector. This will be, from then on, the role I shall act in the play that is being presented. However, the number of masks at my disposal is limited by the situation in which I find myself. My servitude resides in this, as an existence determined by the circumstance in which it finds itself. The circumstance called "Western civilization," in which I find myself, offers a relatively large quantity of masks, if compared, for example, with the situation called "Andaman culture." My circumstance is, in this sense, more open, and offers more freedom. However, an observation of my circumstance makes it obvious that it tends to become progressively restricted. Today this circumstance no longer offers as many masks as it did, for example, in the Renaissance. And it is possible that it will become entirely restricted to a massifying process, in which the only role to be acted will be the one of the retired functionary. And this perspective adds this: I am relatively free before I choose a mask, before making an existential decision, as it is said in this type of philosophy. Once the decision has been made, I lose my freedom. "Engagement" is the end of freedom. If I chose the existential project called "President of the Republic," if I have authentically made the effort to be the President, I shall never be, for example, a garbage collector. We could extract two divergent existential conclusions from this fact. The first is recommended by Camus, which says that we must act out the maximum number of roles in the play in which we are thrown, although knowing very well that we are only representing a role, and that it is therefore only a pose. In other words, we must be conscious actors, acting a multiplicity of alternative roles. This is what he means when he says that it is necessary to live as much as possible, and not as well as possible. And this is what he means when he says that it is necessary to act a role "*quand-même*," despite the absurdity and pretention of the play. The second conclusion is the one Sartre arrives at. He says that we must dedicate ourselves, in an irrevocable existential decision, to a single mask offered to us by the play. We must realize one mask to its extreme limit, and this is the famous Sartrean "engagement." We must, despite knowing full well that all of it is nothing but the acting of a role, act to the best of our abilities. Sartre elaborates this theme on the "Jewish question," which was, by the way, made into a play by M. Frisch called *Andorra.* If the play, in which I am thrown, offers me the mask "being Jewish," I must dedicate myself to this mask the best I can, even if I am not "Jewish as such," as Frisch's character, called Andri, does. I am Jewish for others and, in the end, I act in function of others. In the end, existentialist thought is nothing but an attempt to unmask the play in which we are all acting. It is not, therefore, by chance that this philosophy appeals so many times to the theatre in order to experientially demonstrate its theses.

So what does this play, in which we find ourselves, represent? It represents myths, and the masks that it offers to us are mythical *personae* that are ritualized in the play. Our existential choice, the choice of being *personae*, is a choice between prefigured mythical characters from the myth that established the play. Our existential projects are prefigured by our myths. For us, to know our myths, is to know ourselves. In this sense, we could say that existentialist thought is a demythologizing thought, but not because it seeks to undo myth, but because it seeks to unveil myth. It is through this attempt to unveil myth that we somehow overcome the circumstance in which we find ourselves. It is through this attempt that we exist in the true sense of the term. The contemplation of the myth that established us here and now, and which established the circumstance in which we are, opens a view for us toward that nothingness from which myth sparked our world and us. It is, in this clear night that opens up before us, in this true reflection ("*Nachdenken*" in Heidegger's words), that things show themselves for what they are: things and not nothingness. The generating and establishing power of myth, this power that Heidegger calls "*welten*" (worlding), is revealed to us through the contemplation of myth. Heidegger says that through this contemplation, nothingness "*west mich an, um sich als Wesen herzustellen.*" Translating, I could say that through this contemplation, nothingness presents itself to me in order to become established as an entity. And myth is the form of this "*Anwesenheit,*" of this presence of nothingness. Myth is always "*anwesend,*" it is always present and establishing, because it is through myth that nothingness establishes itself as entity. Today, ontology is, in the end, mythology.

It is necessary to existentially analyze how and in which climate nothingness presents itself to me, "*mich anwest,*" when I contemplate myth. We have already spoken of this analysis. It is through poetry that myth appears as the establishing articulation of nothingness as something. The method, through which myth is established, is the method of poetry, and the poet is the mouthpiece that articulates nothingness. In this sense, the poet is the mouthpiece of the gods, and it is in this sense that God speaks through the prophets' mouths. The Greek poets invoke the muses, and this is not a simple pose, but a confession that the poets are instruments of the power that sparks worlds. That is how we should attempt to comprehend the Greek term "*musiké techné*": the arts through which worlds are established. There is a deep correspondence between music and mathesis, and this deep correspondence relates to the logos. Musical harmony and mathematics are the climate in which the Greek myth emerges, and this is the basis for logic. It is Pan's flute that establishes, with its mathematical harmony, what we call "reality." And the climate, in which this establishing of reality happens, is the Panical terror of the articulating gods. It is also the Orphic chant, through which Orpheus, such Panical incarnation, becomes free from the "*kyklos geneseos*" of the Nietzschean eternal return of the same. Greek art and philosophy, starting with Pythagoras and culminating in Christianity, is the ritualization of this Panical myth that tells of the myth's emergence. And when the prophets say "*omar veomer Adonai*" (God speaks and speaks), it is not an empty phrase: They confess that they are nothing but instruments of the power that sparks worlds. God created the world through the word that gave the spark, He said, "let there be light," and there was light through the Divine word. The world was nothing more than the Divine word realized. This is the "*Ruach Hacadoch,*" the sacred breath, the Holy Spirit, which establishes the world in the form of myth. The Greek poets and the Jewish prophets knew that, in their act of self-awareness, they were mere vehicles of this Holy Spirit, this *pneuma*. And what of today's poets, do they not find themselves in a parallel situation? Do we not also have the sensation of inspiration when we authentically confront that nothingness from which myths irrupt? Myths continue to be revealed, and to establish worlds, from and through the poets. Myth is not something that happened in a historical and remote past. Myth is what is established "*in illo tempore*," that is, always and forever. Myth is always "*anwesend*," its sparking power is always present, and it is present through the poets. The poets are our mouths, through which we extract myths from the nothingness that surrounds us, and which infiltrate our existences from all sides in order to problematize them. The great Czech poet Vítězslav Hálek says, "*Ten národ ještě nezhynul, dokud mu věštec zpívá, a píseň v nebi zrozená i ve smrt život vlívá.*"[8]

This always-imminent occurrence of the myth, with its vivifying power, like a renewing rain that precipitates upon the arid and prosaic plain, in which we exist, rips open our compact and nauseating circumstance. We are, through these myths, always close to that unarticulated fundament that established the world that surrounds us. The emergence of myths through the poets' mouths prevents the stagnation of the ritual with which we are engaged. Jewish tradition distinguishes between two types of characters in humanity's scene: prophets and priests. Priests keep the ritual of the feast that started from a myth. Prophets reveal new myths to be ritualized as feasts by the priests. In parallel, we could say that the Jewish

---

8. "The people are not yet dead, as long as the prophet sings a song in heaven born, even in death life transforms." *Kdo v zlaté struny zahrát zná* (Whoever plays the golden strings knows) from *Večerní písně* (*Evening Songs*), 1859, set to music by Bedřich Smetana. [TN]

tradition is being kept alive in our current circumstance. Our priests are, for example, the scientists. They maintain the feast that ritualizes myths revealed in bygone times, and they realize these myths through ritual acts, for example, through technology. Our prophets are the poets, as long as we allow a very wide meaning to the term "poet." They establish worlds through their verses, to be ritualized by the priests of the future. These poets prevent, as I see it, the end of our situation, and the exhaustion of subjects from previous myths, or that these should fall into small talk, as some among the existentialists dread.

The circumstance in which we find ourselves could, therefore, be conceived as a feast that ritually fetes, and which is determined by, specific myths. However, there is a point that needs to be highlighted. As it is characteristic of a ritual feast, the participant must not be aware of the fact that he is representing a role in the feast. That is what distinguishes the participant of the feast from the theatre actor. When the Australian wears, in the dance, the kangaroo mask, he does not experience his situation as a ritualized representation. He "really" is the kangaroo. When, in mass, the holy wafer is offered, it does not represent the flesh, it is the flesh. When Newton discovered the laws of mechanics they were not the representation of order, they *were* the order. However, in our current situation, we have begun to discover that we are acting, representing, and that we have become distant from our feast. We have consciously turned into actors. The representative character of our efforts, and especially of scientific effort, our highest ritual, starts to reveal itself. We no longer act as the Australian in the dance, or as the

111

priest in mass, or as Newton in his investigations, but as the actor that represents Hamlet in the scene. There is a schizophrenic quality to our effort. The feast that we celebrate is turning into theatre. The festive character of our circumstance is evaporating, and is being substituted by the character of make-believe. This is the climate of the absurd, which surrounds us, and it explains why some existentialist thinkers say that our society is ending, due to the ultimate realization of the ritual of the feast. A large portion of existentialist investigations, including those investigations called "sociology," is dedicated to the analysis of this phenomenon, of this sudden change in the character of our feast. The awareness of this make-believe is, for example, responsible for that curious "scientism" that stamps a large part of the youth growing up under the signs of the atomic bomb and satellites. In other words, the times we live in lack poetry. The myths that currently emerge as life projects, as openings in the compact mass that surrounds us, are inauthentic myths because they are not extracted in that climate of Panical terror, which characterizes true poetry. Myths such as Brigitte Bardot and Pelé, or Frankenstein and Superman, have the stamp of deliberation and inauthenticity. They are only pale copies of authentic myths such as Ishtar and Apollo, or Hephaestus and Heracles; hence, they cannot give authentic meaning to the existential efforts of our youth. I leave this observation without any comments, since I do not know how to interpret this fact.

You must have noticed that I discussed the problem of myth without framing it in the context of this course. I shall dedicate the next meeting to this attempt, when what I intend to say may become more palpable: that every philosophy is, in the end, a philosophy of language. Today, I only wish to highlight the following: the dominant role that the concept of myth has in today's thought is a danger. It leads, easily, to the glorification of mythical thought to the detriment of civilized thought. It underestimates personal consciousness, and values that obscure Jungian layer of which I spoke earlier. Inadvertently, Nietzsche is the one responsible for this. Significantly, we know that what is called "the myth of the 20th century" is a para-philosophical work upon what could pass as Nazi "thought." However, I do not believe that we can fight this nefarious tendency if we ignore the problematics of myth. The study of myth must have as an aim to elevate mythical thought to the level of enlightened consciousness. After all, is that not what we call "civilized existence"? It is not a case of being for or against myth. It is an attempt to comprehend it, according to the Socratic "*gnothi seauton*," which is, after all, one of our society's fundamental myths. We are, in the end, all dedicated to this effort, including this lecture.

The bibliography is the one I referred to in the course of the lecture.

IX. Proper Name and Myth

The considerations that I submitted to you last Friday, which had myth as a subject, must be reframed within the present lecture. For this I shall resort to J. J. Bachofen's definition, which I have already mentioned and I repeat: "Myth is the exegesis of symbols that articulate the primordial lived experience of a people." This definition is laden with terms that demand to be defined, for example, the terms "lived experience," "primordial," and "people." I shall leave the consideration of these ill-defined terms for a little later and I shall, for now, refine the definition to the following form: "Myth is the exegesis of symbols that articulate something." It is obvious that this definition conceives myth as a linguistic phenomenon, and as you will remember, we have defined "language" as "a set of regulated symbols that articulate something." Our definition of myth states that myth is an exegesis of linguistic phenomena to be defined. What is "exegesis"? According to how it has been applied during this course of lectures, I suggest that the term "exegesis" is synonymous with the term "conversation." I remember that we have sought to define conversation as that linguistic movement that predicates names, and that this predicative movement is an explicatory movement that explicates names, therefore, an exegesis. Effectively, if seen as a whole, conversation presents itself as a movement that begins with proper names that are predicated in the direction of common names. Common names are products of the exegesis of proper names, and conversation is, if seen as a whole, this predicating movement from proper names toward common names. We can, therefore, reformulate Bachofen's definition of myth as follows: "Myth is a conversation that has as its subject, linguistic phenomena yet to be determined."

Bachofen tells us how these linguistic phenomena should be determined: by the terms "lived experience," "primordial," and "people." Let us first consider the term "people." It is obvious that I shall not seek to give you a definition of this term, since it is meaningful in a multiplicity of signifying layers, or, as Prof. Hegenberg said during his last lecture here at the institute, "in a multiplicity of universes of discourse." I shall specify this term only a little within our current discursive universe, by saying that "people" is the place where (or how) a specific conversation occurs. In other words, "people" is how a specific type of conversation occurs. To say that myth is a conversation that has as its subject the linguistic phenomena of a people is a pleonasm. I propose that the term "people" be temporarily eliminated from our attempt to define myth. We shall certainly have to reintroduce this term at a more advanced stage of our effort.

Let us consider the term "lived experience" within the present context. In the original text the term reads "*Erlebnis*," that is, something reached by life, a result of life. I shall not get involved in an argument about the meaning of the term "life," because this would certainly be frustrated. I shall only say that "lived experience" is a term that names the instant that is immediately before the emergence of a proper name, and that it is therefore, an attempt to name something that is external to language. In order to avoid falling into a dry and metaphysical discussion in relation to the extra-linguistic territory, I shall say that the collection of lived experiences is that unarticulated and amorphous whole, or, that collection of virtualities from which proper names emerge. Or, *mutatis mutandis*, I shall say that proper names are articulations of lived experiences not yet articulated. If Bachofen's definition of myth says that myth is a conversation that has lived experiences as its subject, it in effect is saying that myth is a conversation that has proper names as its subject.

At last, let us consider the term "primordial" within the present context. The term "primordial" suggests a first order. The German term used by Bachofen, is "*ursprünglich*," and this term suggests a leap. Please allow me to expand these ideas a little. I shall start from the second law of thermodynamics, which as you know, is the foundational stone of contemporary physics. This law says that, if translated to our context, the collection of entities referred to as "physical nature" tends from a state of order toward a state of disorder, and refers to this tendency as entropy. Disorder has a tendency to increase within physical nature as a whole, as organized systems tend to always diminish. Entropy is equal to zero. The physical world tends toward a final stage of disorganization, referred to by some physicists as "*Wärmetod*," that is, thermic death, which endows the second law of thermodynamics with an existential quality, and which the scientists that formulated it probably did not suspect.

So this is the general tendency of the universe, about which physics engages in discourse. However, there are islands in this universe that denote an inverse tendency. On these islands that are opposed to the general tendency, on these reactionary islands, if looked at from a universal perspective, disorder diminishes and order increases. Entropy can be conceived as the universe's measure of time. Time signifies an increase of entropy. On the islands that I am talking about, time runs inversely. As the physical universe as a whole deforms, these islands inform. The increase of information is the opposite of entropy, it is, as it is commonly referred to today "negentropy." The science that deals with this negentropy, with this reactionary tendency of the second law of thermodynamics, is called "cybernetics," from the Greek root *"kybernetes"* (to drive a rudder). In other words: the science of cybernetics studies phenomena that are opposite to the general tendency in nature. For example: if a cube of salt crystallizes from a solution, this leap, this primordial event, is what cybernetics studies in its aspect of increased information.

So now it must be obvious to you that at the present stage of our argument, "increased information" and "linguistic discourse" are very similar terms, and that basically, cybernetics studies this aspect of language. From the point of view of cybernetics, all of this tendency that is contrary to the second law of thermodynamics, this entire negentropic tendency, is an articulating tendency. Articulation is the opposing tendency to what I have referred to a while ago as unarticulated lived experience. As

118

the proper name articulates the lived experience, it opposes itself to experience and that initiates the predicating movement called "conversation," which is the negentropy of what we may vaguely call "life." Conversation is the negation of life as a set of raw lived experiences. Man as a conservative being, as a thinking being, is opposed to raw lived experiences, and it is in this sense that we may say that within man, conceived in this way, information increases. In this opposition, of man against the entropic set from which he leapt, resides human dignity. Language, as a set of conversations that tend toward an increase of information, is the negative answer to entropy. Man, as a participant of language, is a type of being that says no to the world from which it emerged, and it is via this "no" that the world is forced to establish itself within situations of reality, that is, situations of increased information. Man is primordially "*ursprünglich*," a being that negates entropy; that negates increasing disorder. Given, however, that entropy is a universal tendency, all of this is the same as saying that man is an absurd being.

Let us return to Bachofen's definition of myth, which is our topic. He says that myth is a conversation that has primordial names as a subject, that is, names that leapt from disorder to establish a first order. If we identify "order" with "cosmos," and if we keep in mind what was said in relation to entropy, we may reformulate the definition as follows: "Myths are conversations that have proper names as a subject that establish cosmoi." What is "order" and what is "cosmos?" It is a regulated whole. And of what constitutes this whole? Of symbols that point toward chaos, the disorder from which the regulated system emerged. "Order," and "cosmos," are synonymous with "a set of regulated symbols," therefore, synonymous with "language," as we have defined the term. We can therefore say that myths are conversations that have as their subject, the origin of languages. But as a conversation is in turn a linguistic movement, we must definitely reformulate Bachofen's definition of myth as follows: "*Myths are how languages emerge.*"

Poor Bachofen would certainly be bewildered if he could witness our argument. But we must not forget that one hundred years have gone by since Bachofen formulated this definition, and a lot of conversation has happened in the interim, increasing the information at our disposal, in a challenge to entropy. Therefore, let us step over our scruples for having distorted Bachofen, and let us proceed with the argument. So let us frame it within last Friday's considerations. In order to do that, we must reintroduce the term "people," which we had eliminated. I shall say that a people is the collection of participants of a conversation established by one or more myths. We must, therefore, invert Bachofen's thought. For him, the people are a metaphysical fundament from which myth emerges. Thus, he reveals himself to be particularly Romantic, and in this sense, nationalistic. However, we should say that it is myth that establishes a people. Let us repeat Bachofen's definition: "Myth is the exegesis of symbols that articulate the primordial lived experience of a people." Our argument forces us to say the following: "Myth is the exegesis of symbols that articulate primordial lived experiences in the form of a people." Let us take as an example the already over discussed Andamanese culture. The myth of the let

120

us say "sweet potato" happened "*in illo tempore*," that is, outside of time. There was as symbol, a proper name, which articulated a primordial lived experience called "sweet potato." The exegesis of this symbol, which is the myth of the sweet potato, established an order; a cosmos; a language, which is the Andamanese order; cosmos; language. And as it established this order; this cosmos; this language, it established a people. It is completely meaningless to say that there must have been a people, who articulated this myth. In order to be able to articulate it, they must have had a language at their disposal, which in turn must have been established by a myth, and then we are in a classic regression to infinity. As intellectually unsatisfactory as this may be, and as much as we may intellectually rebel against this barrier established by the term "primordial," we must content ourselves with myth as the spark of both reality, and people. The term "primordial" is a borderline term. It is of no use to wish to go beyond this term. We would only manage to push the origin further into the bottomless pit of the unarticulated, but we would never be able to go beyond the origin. Given the myths that established our civilization, it nurtures faith in a reality that anteceded the origin of the Andamanese myth. This is faith in what we could call "historicism." For us, there was something before the myth of the sweet potato, for example, Darwinian evolution. For us, the myth of the sweet potato is a phenomenon framed within a process. Which is equivalent to say that, for us, the myth of the sweet potato is not a myth. However, for the Andamanese the world emerged with the sweet potato, as it did for us, for example, from a decisive thermonuclear

121

explosion. For the Andamanese, the question, "What was there before the sweet potato?" is meaningless, just as it is meaningless for us to ask, "What was there before the Big Bang?" This is because for the Andamanese, the sweet potato is a myth, and for us, physics is a myth, and myth is what establishes a cosmos.

Our existential projects are realizations of virtualities established by myths. The Andamanese realizes himself in function of the sweet potato myth. We realize ourselves in function of a multiplicity of myths. The difference between a primitive culture and let us say, a complex civilization, resides in this: the Andamanese have few myths at their disposal in order to realize themselves, and we have relatively many at our disposal. We are freer beings, because we have more choices at our disposal. However, at the current stage of our argument, we could specify this difference better. The Andamanese myths established a language whose conversation is relatively impoverished, if compared with the conversations that languages established by our myths allow. For example, the fact that the Andamanese conversation resulted in a single instrument, the bow, while ours resulted in a multiplicity of instruments, is explainable by the relative simplicity of the structure of the Andamanese language. What we call "Andamanese thought" is a relatively simpler process than our own. Nevertheless, it is just as much a cosmic process as ours. The exegesis of symbols that articulate primordial lived experiences results in an order that is just as universal in Andamanese as it is in our languages. Effectively, Western civilization could be framed within the Andamanese world, just as easily as Andamanese culture could be framed within our world. The sweet potato myth explicates everything, including Western civilization, as long as it irrupts into Andamanese culture. Our myths explicate everything, including Andamanese culture, as long as it presents itself to us. This universal all encompassing quality of every language is what allows for translations between languages. Languages are regulated systems of symbols that signify, each on their own, the totality of articulable virtualities. It is clear that the translations allowed by this character of every language, more or less warp the meaning of the original to be translated. For example, if I translate "sweet potato" to "God," or "God" to "sweet potato," I warp their meaning. According to Prof. Miguel Reale, this is so because I have, in the first translation, interpreted the Andamanese world in a Western manner, and in the second case, the Western world in an Andamanese manner. If I properly understand Prof. Reale's concept of "plurality," it is as follows: I have the possibility to change points of view. Or, in order to use Prof. Hegenberg's terminology, I could use the Andamanese language as an object-language of our languages, or I could use the Andamanese language as a meta-language, when our own languages become object-languages.

However, I ask myself if this possibility really does exist, especially in the exemplified case. I ask myself if the Andamanese are really able to interpret their culture from a Western perspective, if they are really able to use our language as meta-language to interpret theirs. I believe that if they do it, the Andamanese will lose faith in their myth and will no longer be Andamanese in the process. The Andamanese, as a being that is engaged in existential realization, which is a project against entropy, is a being that is engaged in a specific myth. He cannot authentically overcome such myth without losing himself in small talk. The same applies, *mutatis mutandis,* to our own efforts and myths. I do not know, it is true, of any case of a Westerner seeking to interpret Western myths in the Andamanese manner. However, there are many well-known similar cases, as for example, the case of Zen Buddhism in the United States. And this attempt to leap out of the myths that established our world – and ourselves as thinking beings within a specific set of languages – seems to me to bear the stamp of inauthenticity. If this argument is correct, this is severely limiting for Prof. Reale's "plurality," as it limits the possibility to transform object-languages into meta-languages; as it limits the possibilities of translation, or in other words, it limits human freedom. If I am correct, we are beings who are severely limited by the myths that established our worlds and us. In this sense, I would like to once again mention the image used in the last exposition, of the masks at our disposal, and of the roles that we are called upon to act on stage, and the rebellion against it, which to me, seems frustrated.

Allow me to mention, in this context, the thought of Vicente Ferreira da Silva. For him, the structure of our myths corresponds to the structure of our phrases, which is something that he only became aware of after having had contact with me. He called this structure "subject-form" [*sujeitiforme*]. According to him, we are thrown into a world in which we are subjects, and all of our moves are directed against our circumstance in a gesture of hate against the world. Due to this hatred that we nurture for the world, the world is transformed into a manipulable, and therefore, annihilable object. The structure of our myth will have been realized, when the world we hate has been entirely manipulated, therefore, when that stage our myths call, the "fullness of times," has been reached. This eschatological and paradisiac stage is about to be reached, by two of the more developed societies, the Soviet Union and the United States. Vicente Ferreira da Silva fought desperately against this tendency in our society, thinking that maybe we would be able break the fence that our myths established around us, which he identified as Christianity. He sought openings toward other myths, for example, from Olympic Greece, or Africa, or ancient Germany. But he knew, intimately, of the failure of his attempts, hence, his pessimism.

I believe that this type of thought is in a vice at its base. It disconsiders, or does not know, the negentropic tendency of every language, such as it was sparked by the myth, or myths, that established them and which tend to increase the informative content of languages. But it is true that this process is accompanied by another distorting process, which cybernetics calls "noise," and we, in our context, have called "small talk." And undoubtedly, there are phases in the linguistic process, such as the current one, in which small talk seems to overcome conversation so that the entire conversation seems to be directed toward exhaustion, similarly to the entropic process. Societies such as the Soviet and American ones may really seem, sometimes, to serve as examples of the thermic death that the second law of thermodynamics suggests. However, the fundamental structure of language, which in the case of our languages is the predication of proper names toward common names, fundamentally guarantees language as a negation of entropy. Through conversation, predication increases information, regardless of the amount of small talk that accompanies it. In order to transfer this argument to the field of myths, we could say that the structure of language is such that the impulse it receives from myth is inexhaustible. Formally, we could prove this affirmation by the fact that the meaning of every proper name is inexhaustible through predication. Far from our myths coming close to an ultimate realization; far from Christianity being currently realized through technology as a realization of an Earthly Paradise (to mention Vicente Ferreira da Silva); what is being exhausted, if so, are only a few aspects of Christianity, or, those aspects that deal with the exact and applied sciences. Our myths are inexhaustible, and our history proves it. The lived experience of poetry also proves it, whose existential aspect I have already sought to analyze with you. We are always in touch with myths. Effectively, poetry is an exegesis of symbols that articulate lived experiences (to return to Bachofen), although these lived experiences are perhaps not as primordial as the lived experiences from which they were established. Poetry guarantees, therefore, that the myths that sparked our conversation continue to always be operative. Or, as I said in my last exposition, poetry guarantees that myths are always "*anwesend*," that is, always present and establishing realities. In other words: because the poets are always close to, and open to myths, our language is always renewed through poetry. Our age, the current phase of our conversation, is characterized (and here Vicente Ferreira da Silva is correct) by symptoms of exhaustion. However, this exhaustion only relates to layers of meaning (or universes of discourse) that are more evident today. On other layers, there is a process of poetic reformulation of our myths, which opens a whole gamut of new informative investments. Thought in general, and Western thought in particular, is a process that negates chaos, and this negation is as limited as chaos itself.

What Vicente Ferreira da Silva said can also be applied, in a certain way, as an argument against the pessimism that characterizes today's existentialist thought. Impressed by the symptoms of exhaustion, which characterize the current Western conversation, existentialist thinkers tend to assume anti-intellectual positions. They tend to find refuge in direct experience, which is, obviously a betrayal of human dignity. They dive into myth. But not in order to hurl themselves against it in a predicative exegetic movement, therefore with thought, but in order to become mute within it, within what they call "mythical thought" (or any other analogous term). I believe that an existential analysis of language overcomes this type of anti-intellectualism. I confess that my interest in the study of language is motivated, in large part, by this attempt to prevent the loss of the intellect, which threatens to happen to us at this stage of the conversation. It is obvious that we live in a transitional moment, that is, at a moment when the universe of the predominant discourse finds itself about to become exhausted and substituted by another. Allow me to end this exposition with a verse by

127

Rilke: *"Jede dumpfe Umkehr der Welt hat solche Enterbte, / denen das Frühere nicht und noch nicht das Nächste gehört."*[9]

---

9. "Each sluggish revolution of the world leaves its dispossessed-heirs neither of things past nor of those impending." From the *Duineser Elegien* (The Duino Elegies), 1922. Trans. Robert Hunter. [TN]

X. The Verb

First I shall attempt to summarize the path we have followed up until now before again picking up the thread from where we left off: what Western tradition refers to as "thought," or "spirit," has been represented, under my analysis, as a field in which words occur, organized by certain rules. These rules are the field's structure; they are like imaginary lines on which words occur. We may distinguish roughly three types of fields, that is, three structures on which words occur: the fusional (or inflective), the agglutinative, and the isolating ones. In the fusional field, words occur within structures called "phrases," which have a predicative form, that is, a *"Gestalt"* called "project." If we consider this type of phrase a little closer, we can see that it consists of three groups of words. The first group forms around a name and is called "subject," the second forms around a verb and is called "predicate," and the third also forms around a name and is called "object." Names and verbs are like the building blocks of the phrase, and the remaining words are like mortar. In order to distinguish building blocks from mortar, we can say that names and verbs are referent words, and that the rest are structural words, or, since the structure of our field is called "logic," they are logical words. The phrase is a project that projects verbs from names to names through a predicating slope called "discourse." At the summit of every discourse there is a proper name, which is the first subject of every discourse. The remaining names that occur in the discourse are common names. Common names result from the predication of proper names and refer to these. The meanings of common names are proper names, and it is in this sense that they are referent words. Proper names refer to something that is pre-linguistic, which we may refer to by any term, for example "lived experience," or "becoming," or "nothingness." In order to frame my argument within the body of existential philosophy, I have decided to call what proper names refer to as "nothingness." The meaning of proper names is nothingness, and it is in this sense that proper names are referent words. Verbs establish relations between names, that is, they establish what Neopositivism refers to as "*Sachverhalt*" (objective relation) and which Existentialism refers to as "*Bewandtnis*" (actual situation). The meaning of verbs is the situation and it is in this sense that they are referent words. It is as if logical words were the *detritus* of verbs that refer to already established situations. Therefore, they guarantee the discursive flux since they join phrases to one another in chain-links called "arguments." They are not, in this sense, referent words. All words are symbols; entities that signify something, point to something, and substitute something. Words are symbols of the discourse, verbs are symbols of the situations established by discourse, common names are symbols of proper names, and proper names are symbols of nothingness. The collection of all symbols is called "language." Thought, the field in which languages occur, is signifying. Several types of phrases can occur within this signifying field. Phrases that consist of verbs that establish names within discursive situations will be called "correct" phrases. Phrases that contain verbs, that establish names within situations, whose continuous discourse leads toward a non-discursive situation and therefore force an end to the discourse, will be called "incorrect." Lastly, phrases occur in which verbs do not establish names in situations and these will be called "meaningless." Discourse could be understood as the process that distinguishes between phrases that are correct and phrases that are incorrect, thereby eliminating the incorrect ones. Meaningless phrases are not really part of the discourse since they infringe upon the rules of the field in one way or another. They are not proper thoughts, but are what logic and cybernetics refer to as "noise" and Existentialism as "small talk." As a process to eliminate noise, discourse can be considered as an informative process that is opposed to entropy. As a process to eliminate incorrect phrases, discourse can be considered as a process of progressive knowledge. If we contemplate discourse as a process to eliminate incorrect phrases, it will become clear that the term "incorrect" is relative to a given stage of discourse. A phrase is incorrect only when, at a given stage of discourse, it becomes revealed as such by discourse itself. At a given moment of discourse, all discoursed phrases are correct, in the sense of lending themselves to be discoursed. There are phrases that are eliminated very quickly from discourse, and these can be referred to as "obviously incorrect." There are others that demanded, if looked at historically, complex arguments in order to be eliminated. And there are others that continue to be discoursed. These are called correct phrases until they can be eliminated as being incorrect. The tendency of the discourse is to discourse correct phrases until they are revealed as being incorrect. This tendency can be referred to as "doubt," and discourse as a whole can be referred to as the process of progressive doubt. The aim of this process is the elimination of all phrases. Thought is therefore a negentropic process, because it eliminates noise and increases information, and it is an eliminating process because it tends toward exhaustion. In short: thought is a negating and negative process. What thought negates is the nothingness that proper names signify. Thought is a process that negates nothingness.

The individual correct phrases, which in their totality amount to the body of the discourse at a given moment, are the individual stages of this negation of nothingness. Every individual correct phrase establishes, within this negation, a situation of reality, and as a whole, that is, as the discourse of a given moment, they establish a cosmos. I shall call "reality" the collection of all the situations established by correct phrases. "Reality" becomes a discourse. Our reality is different from the reality of the Andamanese discourse, and different from the reality of the 19th century. It is different from the Andamanese reality because our phrases establish situations with different structures. And it is different from the 19th century reality because several phrases have been eliminated as incorrect by our discourse. Another aspect of the same process is that phrases establish "Selves." Selves are like imaginary points where phrases crisscross within the field of thought. We can conceive thought as the field in which phrases cross through Selves, or, *mutatis mutandis*, as the field in which Selves are linked by phrases. In this aspect, thought reveals itself as a conversation between Selves. "I" becomes a concept relative to conversation, that is, I am because I think, or I am as I am because I converse as I converse. In other words, I realize myself conversing. If I bring together both aspects of discourse synthetically, I can say that I am because I realize a cosmos in conversation with other Selves. In other words: I am here as a negation of nothingness and I find my "Self" as I find myself in a circumstance that consists of situations that negate nothingness. Seen through this prism, nothingness is synonymous with death, because death is for me what nothingness is for the proper name, that is, the ulterior meaning. I am here as a negation of death and it is in conversing that I negate death. Conversation is my negating answer to death. Conversation is my immortality. Death, being the ulterior meaning of the Self, is, under this aspect (the existential aspect), the spring that propels discourse. To reformulate: discourse, if looked at formally, starts at the proper name, which signifies nothingness, and if looked at existentially, starts at the Self, which signifies death. In sum, proper names are confused with Selves and objectivism is confused with subjectivism.

Thought — as the field in which phrases that establish situations of reality and Selves occur, that is, as a field that negates nothingnes — can be compared to a fluvial system that springs from several sources, brings together these tributary influences into several rivers and ramifies the course of these rivers into several branches. I have called the sources "myths," the force that makes them spring "poetry," the tributary influences "verse," the several rivers "prosifying critique," and the several branches "arguments." Myths are the way in which proper names originally appear within thought. These proper names, established by the poetic force of myths, are the subject to be conversed. They are the culminating point from which the slope of discourse starts. Proper names established in myth are what is doubted. Doubt starts at mythical proper names and realizes itself through their progressive predication. The consequences of doubt in myths are on one hand a cosmos and on the other, Selves. Proper names, which appear in myths, vibrate in sympathy with the nothingness from which they emerged and which they signify. This vibration is what we call "truth." In other words: truth is the relation between the proper name that appears in myth and what the proper name signifies. Truth is unthinkable, because it is prior to thought, although it is a quality of thought. Effectively, truth is the poetic quality of thought. The results of the first predication of these proper names that appear in myths are phrases called "verses." Verses are phrases that have a subject for a primordial proper name established by a myth. Verse is an original phrase, and in this sense, real, because it is in sympathetic vibration with the articulated "no." "Truth" and "originality" are therefore synonyms. Doubt, as the slope of the discourse, submits these original and truthful phrases to a progressive critique by transforming them into correct phrases with the intent of eliminating them as incorrect phrases. Some verses can be quickly eliminated by critique, and the conversion of verse into

134

prose demonstrates that these verses are not original. Critique can prove the inauthenticity of the verse, that is, its falseness. Lack of originality is synonymous with falseness. False verses do not give origin to discourse in the strict sense of the term. Other verses cannot be exhausted so quickly. These are the ones that spring from authentic myths. The authenticity of a verse can be measured by the extension of the discourse that it initiates. Given the continuity of the discourse, some verses have, up until now, been revealed as inexhaustible. Effectively: the myths from which these verses have sprung are the subjects of our discourse, and established what we call "reality"; that, in which, we find ourselves. We are here in virtue of these myths. And given our openness to death, we are in contact with these revealing myths in two ways. Through the discursive method, since myths have established our reality, and through the introspective method, since myths are "*anwesend*" (present) in our vacuity called death. The introspective method, which is a dive into our vacuity, is poetry. Through poetry we come into immediate contact with the myths that have established us. Through poetry we regain contact with the truth. Myth always re-establishes itself within the solitude where we face death. Through poetry we re-establish contact with our sources. Our reality is absurd, in the literal meaning of the term, that is, "distant from the roots." In the loneliness of poetry we rediscover our roots and overcome the absurd. In this context I draw your attention to the concept of "music" in the body of Schopenhauer's thought. I shall return later to this concept. Such vacuity of death allows us to always return, to always renew the discourse, and to prevent its stagnation. Death is a constant inspiration for this. We continue to think, because we continue to negate death. And we negate death by facing it and by including it at every instant of thought. To face and to negate death is synonymous with poetry. In facing and negating death, we avoid the transformation of discourse into prose. We avoid the absurd. Truth – which presents itself to us as we face and negate death, and at the moment of poetic inspiration – has a climate of enigma. The verse that establishes itself within us and through us at the moment of poetic inspiration has a double quality, and this double quality causes the verse to be enigmatic. In some ways we recognize the verse as being ours and in other ways we do not recognize it to be so. What is ours within the verse is the discourse in which we participate. What is not ours within the verse is its vibration with nothingness. This enigmatic quality of the verse is its meaning. The critique that will convert verse into prose exhausts the enigmatic quality of the verse. Conversation is an explication of enigmas. Conversation is a deciphering of verses. Verses are the cyphers that conversation decodes. All of the information in the discourse is already contained within the cyphers that verses are. Conversation, as it deciphers these verses, unfurls such information in the form of cosmoi and Selves. It explains and turns the information into prose, and "prose" comes from "*prorsus*" (plane). The conversation's slope is the explication of enigmas, and its aim is a stage where there are no enigmas. The lack of enigmas is synonymous with the absurd. The aim of conversation is the absurd. Existence exists on a slope that starts at the enigma and points toward the absurd. The most rigorous

136

conversation and the one that currently progresses the most, is the one of the natural sciences. Let us consider this conversation within the current context. I shall take as a basis Prof. Hegenberg's most recent book[10] and I shall say the following: the natural sciences are a conversation that consists of several types of explications. Deductive and probabilistic explications characterize the branch called "physics," teleological ones characterize the branch called "biology," and genetic ones characterize the branch called "social sciences," however, this classification is obviously not rigorous. We may disagree with this classification, indeed, as I disagree, but as a basis for the argument it will work. The subject of the conversation called the natural sciences, is the same, that is: specific verses articulated by specific myths. Within the current context, it may be preferable to refer to these as "observations," as long as we keep in mind that "observation" is a real initial situation prefigured by myth. As verses, observational phrases are true, unless they become unmasked, by critique, as being inauthentic, that is, false. For example: the observational phrase "I saw a centaur" is false, because it contains a proper name that has already been conversed and eliminated as being part of an incorrect situation. However, this observational phrase was true within another context, within a different reality. Not being original in the current context, it is eliminated. The observational phrase "I have seen the trace of a proton" is accepted as being true, for being an original verse that is derived from a current myth. Within another context it may be rejected as false. But there is a curious thing. My conversation will

10. *Introdução à Filosofia da Ciência*. São Paulo: Herder, 1965.

accept this observational phrase as true, however, it will tend toward doubting this phrase, by explicating it, with the aim of eliminating it as false. Thus it is the starting point for the conversation called "the natural sciences." To accept phrases as being true and to doubt them at the same time is what is referred to as the ambivalence of science, or as an empirical and rational argument at the same time. As I have already dealt with this difficulty, and as it is precisely one of the sources of the philosophy of language, I shall not deal with it in the present context. According to Prof. Hegenberg, I can doubt the verse "I have seen the trace of a proton" in four different ways. For example, I can ask "why?" in two different ways, and thus the world of physics will emerge. I can ask, "what for?" and thus the world of biology will emerge. I can ask "how?" and thus the world of sociology will emerge. As you can see, all the different sciences do not distinguish themselves by subject, but by the method through which the subject is doubted and how it attempts to explicate it. The same original situation, in our case the situation established by the "observational" phrase "I have seen the trace of a proton," can originate an argument within physics, biology, sociology and (I add) a whole series of other arguments. In other words: every science explicates the reality established by our myths, although each individual science does it in its own way. Every individual science deciphers the information within original verses, although each individual science does it in its own way. Once the verse is deciphered, and the information within it explicated, the original enigma disappears and the absurd emerges. Every individual science is an argument aimed at explicating the information cyphered in the verse, in order to transform the original enigmatic climate into a final climate of absurdity. In other words: every individual science is an interpretation of original verses that generate reality. Therefore: as original verses, phrases that have proper names as subjects can be interpreted in diversely infinite ways. There are an infinite number of possible explications for the reality established by these verses. The natural sciences represent only three or four possibilities within this infinite gamut of possibilities. As every individual science explicates reality as a whole, we have the erroneous impression that this is a definitive explication. However, this pretension toward absolutism, held by every individual science, is contradicted by the arguments of other sciences and other discursive disciplines. If we give any credit to this pretension, we fall into those absolutist worldviews ("*Weltanschauungen*"), such as Mechanism, Biologism, Psychologism and Socialism. If we keep in mind the plurality of interpretations, these conflicting absolutisms will cease to frighten us. We are in a similarly tolerant situation as that of the Enlightenment, which compared the dogmas of different religions in order to free itself from all dogmas. I am particularly thinking of *Nathan the Wise* by Lessing. The plurality of sciences, each claiming for itself the absolute authority as the "interpretation of reality," is experiential proof of science's erroneous pretension, as a whole, to be the "correct interpretation" of reality.

Seen from this angle, the current stage of the scientific argument, which characterizes in such a significant way the situation in which we currently find ourselves, becomes less terrifying. It is true that some among the scientific arguments, especially the one called "mechanist," have reached a highly interpretative degree and have surrounded themselves with the climate of absurdity that is so familiar to us. The situations of secondary reality that these evolved arguments establish around us, and which are characterized by the term "instruments," effectively constitute prosaic situations that threaten to extinguish the discourse's subject. But they are nothing more than a few among the infinite number of possible interpretations. The technological world that surrounds us is only one among the infinite possible outcomes of our myths. If, at this level of interpretation, the argument seems to edge toward an end, this does not mean, necessarily, the end of discourse. It only means that the natural sciences, as an argument to explicate and interpret our reality, have a tendency to wane its existential interest and that this interest tends to transfer to other interpretative levels. We are at a stage of our discourse where there is a transfer of interest. It is obvious that this transfer of interests causes a transvaluation of values. The dilemma of our situation resides in the fact that traditional values are almost emptied out, without having until now managed to exchange them for others. However, the inexhaustibility of our originating myths and our possibility to always come into contact with them through poetry, seems to guarantee that the transfer may happen.

I do not intend, with these considerations, to deny the dramatic quality of the moment. It is obvious that the present moment demands from each one of us a painful expansion of consciousness, since it demands from each one of us a confrontation with death at every instant. What I intend, is to simply show why the desperate pessimism of existentialist thinkers seems unjustified to me. Existentialism is a stage within that discourse referred to as "Western civilization," conditioned by the climate of absurdity that surrounds the advanced arguments of the natural sciences and their instruments. But I believe it to be a stage that can be overcome, and which is, effectively, on its way to being overcome. The confluence that currently delineates between the formal philosophy of language and existential philosophy, which in the end, is also a conscious philosophy of language, represents in my view, one of the most promising symptoms of this possible overcoming.

You will have noticed that I have dedicated this lecture to a summary of all the positions until now adopted. I have not kept the promise to consider Schopenhauer, and I leave this discussion to future opportunities. Effectively, I have reached today in my argument, a culminating point. I consider the very basis of my thought to have been exposed. In the following lectures of this course I propose the application of these bases to the reality referred to as "the history of thought." I propose, in other words, that we start from now on the discussion of our thought "made concrete." As a first step, I propose a discussion of Jewish thought, and the way in which it continues to act today, as a force that molds our reality and us.

Univocal Publishing
411 N. Washington Ave., STE 10
Minneapolis, MN 55401
www.univocalpublishing.com

ISBN 9781937561536
This work was composed in Berkely and Trajan.
All materials were printed and bound
in July 2016 at Univocal's atelier
in Minneapolis, USA.

The paper is Hammermill 98.
The letterpress cover was printed
on Crane's Lettra Fluorescent.
Both are archival quality and acid-free.

Flusser Archive Collection